MEDIEVAL REALMS

Mark Hubbard

Roger Knill

Philip Allan Updates
Market Place
Deddington
Oxfordshire
OX15 0SE

Orders
Bookpoint Ltd, 130 Milton Park, Abingdon, Oxfordshire, OX14 4SB
tel: 01235 827720
fax: 01235 400454
e-mail: uk.orders@bookpoint.co.uk
Lines are open 9.00 a.m.–5.00 p.m., Monday to Saturday, with a 24-hour message answering service. You can also order through the Philip Allan Updates website: www.philipallan.co.uk

Design by Neil Fozzard.

Printed in Great Britain by CPI Bath.

Environmental information
The paper on which this title is printed is sourced from managed, sustainable forests.

Contents

The battle for the crown of England

The Bayeux tapestry

The picture below is a famous scene from the Bayeux tapestry, an important piece of historical evidence. It is like a still from an action film. Can you work out what is happening in it?

The Bayeux tapestry was made by the English who were famous for their tapestry making at this time. However, the tapestry was paid for by the Normans to celebrate their victory over the Saxons at the Battle of Hastings on 14 October 1066.

The Bayeux tapestry is the closest thing there is to an animation of the battle. It is about 70 metres long and 50 centimetres wide. As you can see from the other pictures on pages 4–5, it tells the exciting story of a battle that the Normans won despite overwhelming odds.

The two sides

The battle was fought between William, the Duke of Normandy, and Harold Godwinson, the Earl of Wessex. The prize was the crown of England. Both men believed that they had the right to rule England and were prepared to fight to the death to prove their claim.

This is a scene from the Bayeux tapestry. The tapestry was produced in 1077 and was paid for by the brother of William the Conqueror, Bishop Odo, the Bishop of Bayeux

Helmet (no noseguard)

Round shield

Battleaxe (double bladed)

Sword

Tunic (no chain mail)

A Saxon housecarl

The Normans

William's army was about the same size as Harold's, but all his soldiers were well trained and well armed. It included:

- ❖ archers
- ❖ slingers (men who fired stones using a sling)
- ❖ cavalrymen
- ❖ infantrymen (foot soldiers) with spears and swords

Helmet (with noseguard)

Long bow and arrow

Chain-mail tunic

Sword

A Norman archer

Helmet (with noseguard)

Spear

Hauberk (chain-mail tunic)

Tapering long shield

Broadsword

Mace

A Norman cavalryman

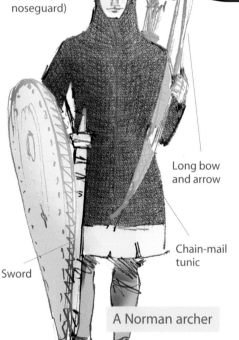

The arrows and stones could kill from a distance, the cavalrymen could attack quickly and the infantrymen could get in close. This meant that William could vary his tactics in the battle.

William also brought about 4,000 other men, including blacksmiths, armourers and cooks, to support his invading army.

The Saxons

Harold, Earl of Wessex, led his army to the top of Senlac Hill, near Hastings, where he waited for the Norman attack. Harold was confident in his army, which was a mixture of 500 well-armed, well-trained housecarls and about 6,500 less well-trained fyrd.

Although Harold's soldiers did not all have the protection of a coat of chain mail (known as a hauberk), they did have shields. They planned to use their shields to form a 'wall' to protect their leader. This was the key to their tactics in the battle.

Activity

❶ Copy and complete the following table.

	Saxons	Normans
Advantages		
Disadvantages		

❷ Which side do you think won the battle? Why?

❸ What other factors might affect the outcome of a battle like this?

The Battle of Hastings

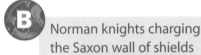

To see how each side used its advantages we need to look at the battle itself.

Harold's advantages

At first, the battle went Harold's way. The Normans had to attack uphill to dislodge the Saxon housecarls, but they were continually repelled by the Saxons. Their arrows bounced off the shield wall.

There was even a rumour that William was dead. To rally his troops and prove the rumour wrong, William took the risk of removing his helmet in the middle of the battle and said: 'Look at me well! I am alive and by God's grace I shall yet be victor.'

The Normans found it very difficult to break the wall of shields. They realised that they had to force it to break if they were to have any chance of winning the battle.

William's tactics

The Normans noticed that when their cavalry chased up to the shield wall, some housecarls and fyrd chased after the cavalrymen. William thought that if his soldiers could pretend to retreat and draw more men down from the high ground, onto the level ground, then the superior trained men of the Norman army would be able to slaughter the less well-armed English fyrd.

B Norman knights charging the Saxon wall of shields

This clever tactic worked. Once the wall of shields was broken, Harold's army could not protect him so well and the Norman archers were able to get near to him. Harold's troops formed an ever smaller circle to protect him, but, despite a brave fight, he was killed. The Bayeux tapestry shows Harold being shot in the eye with an arrow (see page 2).

Activity

❶ Pictures **A** to **E** are from the Bayeux tapestry, but they are in the wrong order. Read the story again and put the pictures in the right order.

❷ Look at pictures **A** to **E** again. You need to write two captions for each picture:

❖ Your first caption for each picture should describe what the Normans might have said was happening in it.

❖ Your second caption for each picture should describe what the Saxons might have said was happening in it.

Write your captions in two different colours to make it easier to tell them apart.

D William removing his helmet

A Saxons running away

Activity

❸ Look at the list of reasons why William might have won the battle:
  a well-trained Norman soldiers
  b William's determination to win
  c bravery of the Norman soldiers
  d William's bravery in the battle
  e good leadership skills in the battle
  f lack of trained soldiers in the Saxon army
  g variety of weapons in the Norman army
  h fighting on foreign soil
  i variety of types of soldiers the Normans had

Give each reason a score out of 5 to show how important it was in explaining why William won the battle (1= not very important; 5 = very important). Are there any factors in the list that might have made it harder for William to win?

C Preparations for the battle

E Norman knights killing the Saxons on level ground

Did William deserve to win the battle?

William was a skilled tactician as well as a brave and determined leader. He was also wise enough to delay his invasion until the weather in the English Channel was settled and his boats, laden with soldiers and supplies, could be transported safely. The wind finally changed direction and blew towards England on 27 September 1066.

William's determination

William was determined to succeed. Many of his advisors told him that Harold was too strong and that an invasion would be doomed to fail. Even after a strange comet was spotted in the sky, which many thought was an omen of disaster, he was still prepared to invade England.

Other factors

Was William's victory all down to his skill, determination and genius in battle? Or was Harold a weak leader? Did Harold lack bravery?

Activity

Look at the three decisions boxes and try to decide what Harold should have done in each situation. For each decision, answer the following two questions:

✤ Which was the best option for Harold?

✤ Why were the other options not such a good idea?

Decision 1

Harold knew that William was prepared to attack England. He gathered a huge army and navy to defend the south coast in case of such an attack. They waited all summer but no attack came. In September, some of Harold's soldiers went home to harvest their crops.

On 20 September, something totally unexpected happened. A Viking army led by his brother Tostig and Harold Hardraada invaded Yorkshire. What options did Harold Godwinson have?

1 Leave the Viking invasion to take its course.

2 Split his army in two, leaving some soldiers in the south in case there was an attack by the Normans and sending the rest to Yorkshire to fight the Vikings.

3 Send all his troops to Yorkshire to defeat the Vikings, leaving the south coast undefended.

4 Hope that the northern earls, Edwin and Morcar, would be strong enough and willing to see off the Vikings.

Decision 2

Harold and his men arrived in Yorkshire 5 days later and launched a surprise attack on the Viking army at Stamford Bridge. The element of surprise was vital. Hardraada had not expected the Saxon army to arrive so quickly. The battle was bloody and hard. Both the Viking leaders were killed and many of their soldiers were slaughtered.

Just 2 days later on 28 September, William landed his soldiers at Pevensey on the south coast. What options did Harold Godwinson have?

1 Leave the Normans — their invasion might lack supplies.

2 Send all his soldiers down to meet the Normans in battle, immediately.

3 Let his soldiers rest after such a fierce battle, and then march south and meet William in battle wherever his army had got to.

4 Do a deal with William and let him rule part of England.

Decision 3

Harold faced one last decision. He knew that the Normans had had time to rest. He knew that his own soldiers were too exhausted to fight, but this battle was just as important as the Battle of Stamford Bridge. The Norman army was huge, but it had limited supplies. What options did he have?

1 Attack the Norman stronghold — William had used his time well in preparing for the battle and had built a fortified camp.

2 Choose a defensive position and make the Normans attack him.

3 Do nothing except surround the Normans to try to starve them out.

4 Wait until his soldiers were stronger and he had a bigger army.

You know that Harold took the second option. Could he have done anything different? Was it this decision that lost him the battle?

Key

— Route of Norman invasion

— Route of Viking invasion

→ Route of Harold, King of England

Stamford Bridge

From Norway

Fulford

ENGLAND

London

Pevensey   Hastings

From Normandy

This map shows the two different invasions that Harold Godwinson faced in 1066

Weighing up the evidence

It's time to weigh up your evidence

It's time for you to decide *why* William won the Battle of Hastings. You have looked at some of the factors that helped William and the difficult decisions that Harold had to make before the battle took place. Now you need to decide which were the *most important* reasons.

Harold

William

Activity

❶ Draw some scales in your exercise book. Think back to all the different reasons why William won the Battle of Hastings:

Good tactics	Better weaponry	Good luck
Strong army	Well-trained soldiers	Good planning
Bravery	Great stamina	Good organisational skills
Cunning	Good leadership skills	Any other factors

Decide which of the above factors belongs on which side of the scales. For example, if you think that Harold had a 'strong army', put this on Harold's side of the scales on your diagram. You can use the same factors for both sides, so if you think that William also had a 'strong army' then place it on William's side of your diagram too.

❷ Decide how important each factor was by allocating it a score out of 5 (1 = not very important; 5 = very important). Add these scores to the factors on your diagram.

❸ Look back at your work on the Battle of Hastings. Try to find some factual knowledge to explain why you have put each factor on your diagram. For example, if you thought that Harold had 'well-trained soldiers' you could suggest that this is shown by the fact that they 'held their shield wall for a long time in the battle itself'. Write these explanations underneath your diagram.

Writing history essays

You have studied the events before and during the Battle of Hastings and made judgements about the strengths and weaknesses of William and Harold. This activity is designed to get you to draw your thinking together and to decide what might make a good written piece. It explores how to answer the following question:

William won the Battle of Hastings. Does this mean that he was the best leader?

What makes a good essay?

A good essay must have a clear **structure**: an introduction, a middle and a conclusion.

- **Introduction.** Begin by explaining briefly what you think. For example, do you think William was the best leader?
- **Middle.** This is the main part of your answer. You may need to write more than one paragraph for this part. For example, you could write a paragraph to explain the reasons why William won, followed by another paragraph explaining the reasons why Harold was unable to win. Use your scales to show the importance of each point you make.

Activity

❶ Read 'A first attempt'. This is part of an answer to the question.

  ❖ Which part of the answer is this? Is it the introduction, one of the middle paragraphs, or the conclusion? How do you know?

  ❖ What is the main point it is trying to make?

  ❖ How does it explain the point?

  ❖ What factual knowledge does it use as an example?

  ❖ Is it a clear, well-written paragraph?

❷ How could you *improve* this paragraph? Rewrite it, adding the changes that you think would make it better.

❸ Swap books with your partner. Read their paragraph and decide whether or not they have improved it. Explain to them why it is improved, or how they could improve it further.

❹ Write your own answer to the essay question.

A first attempt

...I think that it wasn't really all William's great skill, in fact I think he was really, really lucky. For a start it would not have happened if the weather didn't change to help him. And the Saxons weren't really ready to fight, so he was lucky there, too. He was also very fortunate that he didn't get his head chopped off when he showed them all his face when they wanted to run away. Really, he was lucky that they saw him in all that chaos of the charging up and down hills in the battle...

- **Conclusion.** End by explaining your decision briefly — don't rewrite your entire answer.

To write a good essay you also need to:

- Make sure that it is **balanced** — look at both sides of the argument and weigh up both sides of the scales.
- Decide how you are going to answer it *before* you put pen to paper — don't change your mind halfway through writing it.

- Make sure that each paragraph has a **P**oint, **E**xplanation and **E**xample (**PEE**).

PEEBS success criteria

Point
Explanation
Evidence
Balance
Structure

What is meant by the 'Norman *Conquest*'?

Read **Source A**. What do you think was happening? What was William doing with guards, meeting a person as influential as an archbishop at a place as important as Westminster Abbey?

Did William conquer England?

William, the Duke of Normandy, definitely won the Battle of Hastings in 1066, but is that enough to enable us to say that he had become the conqueror of England? What do we mean by the word 'conquer'?

To be able to understand what Source A tells us, we need to find out the context of the events. Let's look at what William did straight after his victory at Hastings and the problems that he faced.

Source A

There were guards at the front door of Westminster Abbey as William was greeted by the Archbishop of York. Inside, there were a number of Norman earls and a few Saxon supporters. As the cheers grew, the guards thought that there were problems inside. Immediately, they began to attack the Saxons outside and set fire to the surrounding buildings.

The fire spread quickly, the people inside were thrown into confusion. Crowds of them rushed outside, some to fight the fires, others to take the chance to go looting. Only the monks, the archbishop and a few clergy remained…

William was said to be in a rage inside Westminster Abbey.

Adapted from *The Ecclesiastical History of Ordericus Vitalis*

Fact box

The game of conkers, played by schoolchildren for centuries, is believed to have its origins in the term 'conquer'.

Ordericus Vitalis was written by a monk in the early twelfth century

Thinking aloud

What do you think William should have done about his problems? Are there simple solutions that he could have used straight away?

William's problems

The following were all *immediate* problems for William:
- how to get to London safely
- how to convince the rest of England that he was the rightful king
- how to deal with anyone who refused to accept him as king
- how he should rule England
- what language he should speak

William's solutions

William had to make sure that his army would be safe. It marched to London, taking control of towns like Dover, and burning whole villages on its way. He had decided to use force to control the people.

William also decided that he needed to be crowned king as quickly as possible. He knew that there were other powerful nobles in England, such as **Edwin** and **Morcar** in the north. They may not be ready to accept him as their king. After all, he had only won one battle.

William's claim to the crown

One thing was in William's favour, however. He had what he felt was a genuine claim to the English crown. He claimed that the crown had been promised to him by Edward the Confessor in 1051 (William had helped

Edward defend England against Viking invasion that year).

William also claimed that in 1064 Harold Godwinson had made a sacred **oath** to support him as the next King of England when Edward died. Harold had gone back on this oath. This was why in 1066, when Edward died leaving no **heir** to the throne, William decided to invade

England. Read **Source A** again. Think about how William solved the problems he faced.

25 December 1066

William's victory led him to London and on Christmas Day 1066 the Archbishop of York crowned him King of England in Westminster Abbey. Outside, William's guards were wary; inside, William was impatient. The slightest problem might stop William and lead to the Normans being chased away.

Activity

Throughout this topic you will be looking at power and control. Who was in charge and how did this change throughout the period? Look at the 'controlometer' below.

This is a quick way for us to measure changes in who was in control and how much things changed.

A 'controlometer' to show who had the power

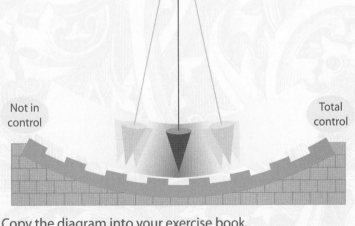

Not in control

Total control

❶ Copy the diagram into your exercise book.
❷ Decide whether or not William was in control. Where might you place the indicator to show how much control he had at this point? Think about how he had got himself into this position and what other dangers he faced.

Gaining control

After winning the Battle of Hastings William had claimed the throne. Now the hardest job was to hold on to the power he had gained.

As soon as the Normans landed at Pevensey they knew that they would have to be ruthless if they were to retain power. As we have seen, even the crowning of William was filled with danger and violence. Some people in England refused to accept him as their king.

Rebellions

There were several rebellions, including ones at Dover in 1067 and Exeter in 1068, but the most fearsome rebels were to be found in the north. Edwin and Morcar, the Saxon earls who had helped out Harold Godwinson at the Battle of Stamford Bridge, were ready to challenge William. They sought help from the Danish king, who sent soldiers.

After a bloody victory at York in 1069 William took steps to stop any further rebellions. His men visited each town and village in the area. **Source A** is an account of what they did.

This cruel revenge by William became known as the '**harrying of the north**'. Did it make him

more secure? Was he stronger as a result?

Look at the picture opposite. It shows **Hereward the Wake**, a famous rebel from the fenlands of Cambridgeshire. The fenlands were marshy and difficult to navigate and so had a natural defence against invasion. But William was determined to crush any resistance to his rule. **Source B** tells part of the story.

Between 1067 and 1075 there were several rebellions in south-east, southwest and northern England. William managed to stop them all, although he never really gained the same control over Wales.

Source B

Edwin and Morcar fled the battle-field and made their way through the woods. Edwin was slaughtered by his own men in the forest, but Morcar arrived in Ely by ship. When William discovered that the rebels were gathered in the Fens he sent his ships and his army to surround the area. He built a causeway and went into the Fens. The outlaw rebels gave themselves up immediately, all except Hereward and his men, whom he led away. William seized ships, weapons and treasure and the men he dealt with as he chose.

Adapted from *The Ecclesiastical History of Ordericus Vitalis*

Source A

…The king himself combed the forests and the remote mountainous places, stopping at nothing to hunt out the enemy hidden there. He cut down many in his vengeance, destroyed the crops of others and burned homes to ashes. This was more ruthless cruelty than he had shown anywhere else. He made no attempt to contain his anger and punished the innocent with the guilty. He ordered that all crops, herds and food should be brought together and burned to ashes, so that everyone north of the Humber should starve. This famine caused the deaths of 100,000 men, women and children.

Adapted from *The Ecclesiastical History of Ordericus Vitalis*

Hereward the Wake, a famous rebel

Activity

❶ It is time to plot the next arrow on your 'controlometer'. Do you think that William increased his level of control, or reduced it by using violence to stop rebellions? Once you have decided, draw another arrow on your diagram — remember, you need to be able to explain your reasons.

❷ **Source A** is about the 'harrying of the north' while **Source B** is about a rebellion in the Fens. What was similar about William's reactions to both these events?

❸ Look at the picture of Hereward the Wake. It was drawn in the nineteenth century, almost 800 years after the event. Do you think it is an **accurate** picture of Hereward the rebel leader? Explain your answer carefully.

❹ Look at **Source B**. It was written by a monk in the twelfth century, about 70 years after the harrying of the north took place. Do you think that this is a more **accurate** source than the picture of Hereward?

❺ Can you think of a long-term problem for William if he continued to rule his kingdom in such a harsh way?

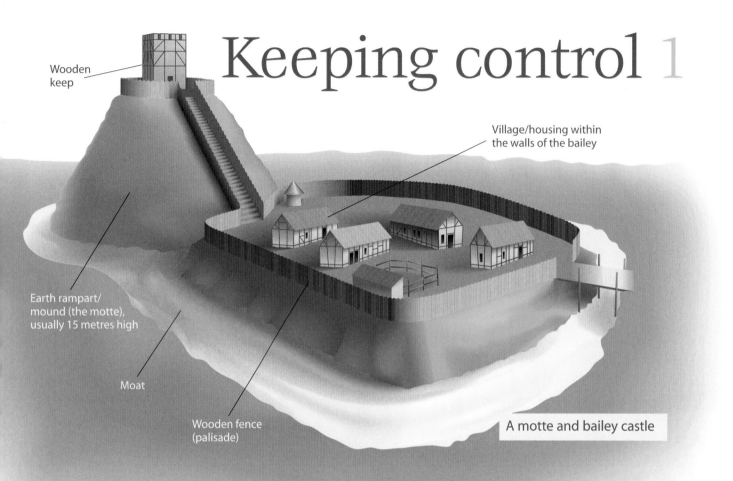

Wooden keep

Keeping control 1

Village/housing within the walls of the bailey

Earth rampart/ mound (the motte), usually 15 metres high

Moat

Wooden fence (palisade)

A motte and bailey castle

William realised that if he was to keep control he had to encourage some key people to support him and help him govern the countryside.

William had a clever four-part plan. Here are the first two parts.

1 Castles

He ordered that castles be built around the country, not only in places where there had been many rebellions, but also in important trading centres. The key to his plan was speed.

Motte and bailey castles (like the one above) were built all over the country, at an average

of four castles per year throughout William's 20-year reign (see **Source A**). This meant that the Norman knights could keep watch over the rebels in their area, and had a fortress to defend if they came under attack. It also allowed William to reward his most trusted knights by giving them an impressive new home. (See Topic 4 to find out more about castles and how they developed.)

2 Land

William decided to share out the land of England with the loyal knights who had helped him at Hastings. They replaced the

Saxon earls, and for many land was the key to power and wealth.

The knights would help keep control, and defend the country from invasion, simply by raising an army in their area. In return for the **reward** of land the **barons** or tenants-in-chief had a **duty** to send William knights for his own army, for 40 days per year (see **Source B**). These were not the only benefits the barons enjoyed. They were also entrusted with the duty of being sheriffs for their area. They kept the fines that they collected and paid the king a fixed sum each year. They also collected taxes from the people in their area.

Activity

❶ Look at the picture of the motte and bailey castle. Can you work out why these types of castle were quick and easy to build?

❷ Look at **Source A**. In which areas of England did the Normans fear rebellions? How do you know?

❸ Can you see any problems for the king or the peasants if the barons were the tax collectors?

❹ It is time to add another arrow to your 'controlometer'. This time, think about the duties of a king. What should a king do for his people? Control them effectively? Protect them? Give them somewhere safe to live? As you place your arrow, ask yourself whether William increased his control or not. Label the arrow.

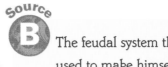

The feudal system that William used to make himself more secure

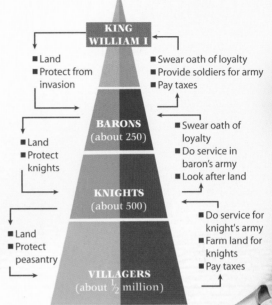

KING WILLIAM I
- Land
- Protect from invasion

- Swear oath of loyalty
- Provide soldiers for army
- Pay taxes

BARONS (about 250)
- Land
- Protect knights

- Swear oath of loyalty
- Do service in baron's army
- Look after land

KNIGHTS (about 500)
- Land
- Protect peasantry

- Do service for knight's army
- Farm land for knights
- Pay taxes

VILLAGERS (about $\frac{1}{2}$ million)

The location of castles built by the Normans

Newcastle
Durham

York

ENGLAND

Lincoln

Nottingham

Stafford
Tutbury

Norwich

Shrewsbury

Warwick

Ely

Worcester

Huntington

Cambridge

Hereford

Colchester

Gloucester

WALES

Oxford

London

Wallingford

Canterbury

Windsor

Dover

Salisbury

Winchester

Bramber

Hastings

Arundel

Lewes

Pevensey

Exeter

Corfe

Totnes

Keeping control 2

We have seen how William used land to gain the support of key people. He used it to control people in other ways too. The third and fourth parts of his plan are explained on these two pages.

❶ Look at the photograph of Durham cathedral. Choose the **six** words from the list below that best describe the building.

Dramatic
Huge
Ornate
Simple
Dark
Impressive
Small
Delicate
Majestic
Elegant
Overpowering
Awe-inspiring

❷ Why do you think the Normans spent *so much* money constructing such grand buildings?

3 Cathedrals

The king gave a lot of land to the Church. The Church was a very powerful organisation. William wanted another way of showing that the Normans were more powerful. He oversaw a huge cathedral-building plan throughout England to replace the smaller, wooden-built, Saxon churches.

The vast stone-built cathedrals dwarfed other buildings in the towns. Winchester, York and Durham are fine examples of Norman cathedrals. They were even bigger and grander than the castles in some places. Imagine how long they took

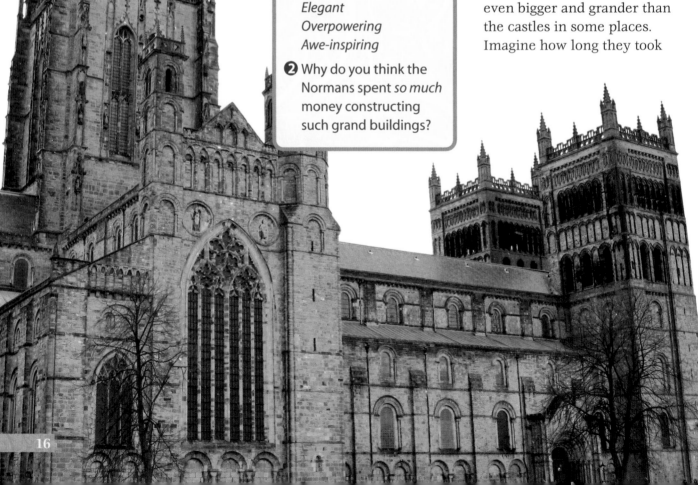
Durham cathedral

to build and how much they cost. William's plan included raising taxes to pay for this grandeur, and the townsfolk were expected to work on the projects too.

4 The Domesday survey

Finally, William decided to find out how much his country was worth. In 1085 he ordered his own officials (rather than the barons) to visit every town and village in England and record what was there. He wanted to know about every item that people owned. It was the most detailed survey that anyone had ever undertaken in England.

The officials asked about:
- who owned the land
- who had held it in 1066
- its size then and in 1085
- how much rent was paid
- how many people lived there
- how much tax should be paid

The officials visited over 13,000 places. It took them a year to complete their visits. Their findings were written up (by hand, as there was no printing press) by a monk in Winchester. The book became known as the '**Domesday Book**'.

Activity

❶ What were William's reasons for carrying out the Domesday survey?

❷ Why do you think that William was keen to choose his own officials, and not the barons, who collected the taxes, to carry out the survey?

❸ Look at the diagram below. The categories all relate to William's plan to control England. There is a link from 'Taxes' to the 'Domesday survey', because William used the survey to find out if he was getting enough tax from his people. There is also a link from the 'Domesday survey' to 'Land' because William was trying to find out who owned which bits of land. How many other links can you make? Make a copy of the diagram in your book and try to make as many links as you can. For each one, number it and note down what the link is.

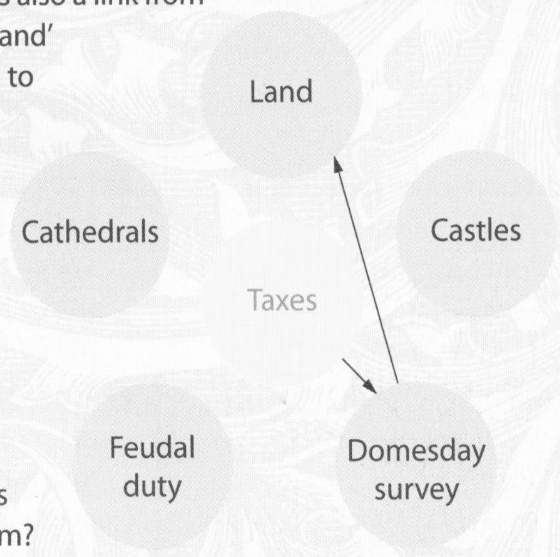

Land

Cathedrals

Castles

Taxes

Feudal duty

Domesday survey

❹ Can you think why 'Taxes' is at the centre of this diagram?

Overview activity

❶ You are now ready to put the final arrow onto your 'controlometer' to show whether William had gained more control or less. How much influence did he have over his subjects after the taxes had been raised to build cathedrals? What impact did the Domesday survey have on William's control over his subjects?

❷ From what you have learned about William, which one of these statements best describes his rule?
   a William was in total control of England by the time he died in 1087.
   b William had bribed people to do as he wanted and that is how he controlled them.
   c William conquered England by the strength of his army alone. It crushed anyone who stood before it.
   d William was a cunning man who used his army to frighten people and his wealth to gain the support of others, and that is how he ruled England.

Choose the 'best-fit' answer and try to find at least **five** pieces of evidence to back up your opinion.

The hierarchy of power

Power and the people who have it or want it can sometimes cause serious problems. In this topic you will be looking at three different problems from three different time periods which faced three different kings. You need to decide who was the most powerful ruler: Henry II, John or Richard II.

First, we are going to look at the clash between the power of the king and the power that the Church seemed to hold over people. The next clash was between the king and the powerful barons. Who was really in charge? Finally, we will look at a king who clashed with the people to see who really held power.

At the end of this topic, you will need to decide what you think happened to the power of the monarchy over the whole period. Did it become more or less powerful?

Starter activity

❶ Look at the diagram below. It is similar to the one depicting William's feudal system (see page 15). Who is the most powerful person? Who has the least power?

❷ There are some groups missing on the diagram. Where would you place the following?
 a Student council
 b School governors
 c Secretary of state for education

❸ If you are at the bottom of the pyramid, how do you get things changed?

Thinking aloud

A hierarchy is a system of ranks. In a hierarchy people are ranked one above another in order of importance. Can you think of any other hierarchies, like in a government or a football club, for instance?

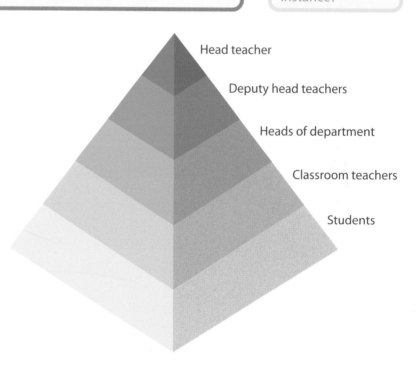

Head teacher

Deputy head teachers

Heads of department

Classroom teachers

Students

Henry II versus the Church (1170)

Henry II became King of England in 1154. He was desperate to gain greater control over the Church. His trusted advisor, **Thomas Becket**, was also his best friend. They hunted, played chess and even sorted out the king's finances together.

Becket as Archbishop of Canterbury

Henry appointed Thomas Becket as Archbishop of Canterbury in 1162. He thought that his friend would help him gain power over the Pope, the head of the whole Catholic Church.

Henry wanted to be able to appoint his own bishops without having to seek the Pope's permission. He also wanted to gain control of the Church courts (see 'Things you need to know', point 1).

But Becket changed. He took his new job seriously. He became deeply religious and defended the Church's rights.

Becket's actions

- Becket failed to support Henry when he passed a law forcing all serious crimes to be tried in the king's court.
- He excommunicated (cut off) barons from the Church.
- He excommunicated all bishops who supported Henry, including the Archbishop of London, Henry's advisor.
- He asked the Pope to punish the Archbishop of York, yet another important churchman who had accepted Henry II's request to crown his son as the next king of England (see 'Things you need to know', point 2).

Henry's reaction

Henry was furious, and was heard by four knights to scream, 'Are you all cowards? Will no one rid me of this turbulent priest?' Almost immediately the knights set sail from France to England.

Henry II

The murder of Becket

Source A

What happened next was unexpected and extremely shocking. The knights found Thomas Becket in Canterbury cathedral. He was praying, surrounded by three monks. **Source A** is an account by a priest, Edward Grimm, who was an eyewitness to the murder.

The murderers came in full armour, with swords and axes....

In a spirit of mad fury the knights called out, 'Where is Thomas Becket, traitor to the king and country?' At this he, quite unafraid, came down the steps and answered, 'Here I am, no traitor to the king, but a priest.' He stood by a pillar.

'You shall die this instant', they cried.

They pulled and dragged him violently, trying to get him outside the church. But they could not get him away from the pillar. Then he inclined his head as one in prayer and joined his hands together and uplifted them.

The wicked knight leapt suddenly upon him and wounded him in the head.

Next he received a second blow on the head, but he still stood firm.

At the third blow he fell to his knees and elbows, saying in a low voice, 'For the name of Jesus I am ready to die.'

The next blow separated the crown of his head and the blood white with brain and the brain red with the blood stained the floor.

The fourth knight warded off any who sought to interfere.

A fifth man put his foot on the neck of the holy priest and scattered the brains and blood about the pavement.

Adapted from Shephard, C. et al. (1991) *Discovering the Past: Contrasts and Connections*

Activity

❶ Read **Source A** and look at the picture of Becket's murder. Can you see where the two agree on details about the murder? Are there any details on which they do *not* agree?

❷ Draw a **storyboard** for a film with four scenes to help you tell the story of how Thomas Becket died. Do not use any words.

❸ Think of a title for your film that would grab people's attention.

❹ An obituary is an account of someone's life and achievements written after they have died. If you were going to write an obituary for Thomas Becket, what would it say?

Skill box

A **storyboard** is drawn by a film director to show the actors the key points in a story. It usually shows the most dramatic points and has no text. Sometimes there is a title for each frame but it's better if each picture explains itself.

The murder scene, from a painting in Canterbury cathedral

Consequences of Becket's murder

After the murder, Henry II was shocked and full of remorse. In 1174 he walked barefoot into the cathedral, knelt before Becket's tomb and ordered monks to whip him more than 200 times. The Pope made Becket a saint, and churches were named after him. Church courts remained for the clergy. The king was, however, still allowed to choose bishops.

Activity

❺ After seeing the long-term results of the falling out of Henry II and Thomas Becket, would you change your obituary in any way?

❻ In this clash between the power of the Church and the power of the monarchy (the king), who won?

King John versus the barons (1215)

Sometimes problems are difficult to solve, especially in situations where people are reluctant to help. Think back to the trouble that Henry II had when he wanted to reduce the power of the Church.

We are going to look at another problem, this time from 1215. By 1199 the king was Henry II's son, **John**. He became king at a time when the monarchy faced many problems.

Starter activity

Is there anything wrong with the way your school week is organised? Hint: think about things like break and lunch times, start and finish times and the length of lessons. Try to think of a solution for each problem. Think who you would need to help you solve these problems. For example:

Problem: The lessons are too long in some subjects (they are 1 hour long).

Solution: Make the lesson a bit shorter.

Who could help?: The head teacher might be able to rearrange the timetable.

You might find it helpful to refer back to the school hierarchy on page 18.

Activity

❶ Copy the following Venn diagram into your exercise book.

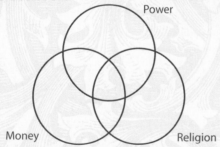

❷ Look at the problems 1–12 which faced King John. Can you sort out which one belongs in which circle? Some problems might fit two different categories, so they can be overlapped.

❸ What do you think was John's biggest problem?

❹ Which people might he have needed to help him?

❺ Look at the following list of solutions that John could have used. Try to match up these solutions to some of the problems opposite.

 a Raise more taxes to pay for more castles to be built on the borders.

 b Increase taxes but only on the barons.

 c Cut off all relations with the Church and appoint his own bishops and archbishops.

 d Raise taxes for everyone and build a navy.

 e Kill anyone who challenged his power.

 f Raise money from taxes to fight wars abroad to increase his popularity.

❻ Why was King John *always* heading for a showdown with his barons?

King John's pressing problems

1 John's brother, **Richard I (the 'Lionheart')**, had defended the Church by fighting in the **Crusades** (a holy war in the Middle East against the Muslim king Sal-A-Din) and everyone thought that he was a great hero. John didn't seem to measure up.

2 Richard had spent vast amounts of money building castles abroad to defend his lands.

3 There was very little money in the treasury.

4 John quarrelled with the Pope over who should become the next Archbishop of Canterbury.

5 After his quarrel with King John, the Pope banned all church services in England. The people feared that they would go to hell if they could not be christened, married or buried by the Church.

6 Some barons refused to pay the 'new' taxes.

7 John's nephew, Arthur, believed that he had more right to the throne.

8 John faced threats of attack from the Welsh and the Scots.

9 The French king, Philip II, wanted to regain some of his lands in Normandy.

10 John fell out with some of his barons over the payment of **scutage**, the money paid by the barons instead of sending knights to serve in the king's army (see William the Conqueror's feudal duty, page 14, for details).

11 John imposed taxes of 'relief' that a baron's son had to pay before he could take over his father's lands.

12 John lost wars to the French in 1214.

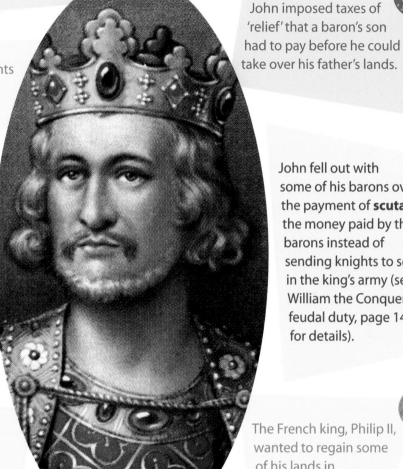

Weighing up the problems

A 'news update' might help you to understand why King John had such problems.

On the negative side

John was suspected of having his nephew, Arthur, killed so that he was no longer a threat. He certainly had the sons of the barons who refused to pay their taxes killed.

In 1213 he had to give in to the Pope, so that the churches could reopen. In 1214 he was defeated by the French. He had increased the rate of tax for some people by more than 500%.

And yet, John was not a complete failure…

On the positive side

He made the system of law and order much fairer. He even tried to be present at trials to ensure that his laws were used properly. He also changed the system of money, which made tax collection easier.

The barons' grievances

Both of these successes took some power away from the barons. Not surprisingly, they had had enough of King John and they began to organise a rebellion.

It nearly spilled over into a **civil war**, but the Archbishop of Canterbury persuaded the barons to make a list of their grievances, which they were to discuss with King John.

The Magna Carta

In 1215, at Runnymede, an island in the Thames, the barons met the king and forced him to accept their list as a set of rules which he had to follow. This set of rules was known as the 'Great Charter' or '**Magna Carta**'.

The barons' new rules for the king to obey

- The king should not interfere with Church business, e.g. he should not choose his archbishop.
- The king should not demand any payment without the permission of the barons and the bishops.
- Barons inheriting land would pay a fixed fee of £100 (not the £500 that John had been desperate to charge).

- All freemen (this really only meant the barons) should have the right to a fair trial, with a jury.
- No freeman could be put in jail without a fair trial.
- There would be no unfair tolls on traders.
- Twenty-five barons would be chosen to meet as the **Grand Council** to advise the king and make sure that he kept to the rules.

John's reaction

What do you think John would have felt about these rules? He actually hated them and signed Magna Carta only to gain himself some respite from the barons.

When he died in 1216 John was once again at war with the

barons. So, maybe Magna Carta was not such a significant document after all. Look at the points below before you make your final decision.

Where the charter came in useful later

- All the kings that followed John used the charter to work with the barons.
- Some parts of the Magna Carta are still part of our civil rights today.
- The US Constitution used some parts of the Magna Carta as a basis for its laws.
- The Declaration of Human Rights signed after the Second World War used some parts of the charter, and it is still used by the United Nations today.

Activity

❶ Who seemed to benefit most from the terms of the Magna Carta?

❷ Do you think the barons were right to make the demands that they made in the Magna Carta?

❸ Can you tell which parts of the charter are still used today?

❹ Read the following statements:
  a The barons failed because the king never really stuck to the agreement in his lifetime.
  b The Magna Carta gave the barons a chance to limit the power of the king; it didn't matter which king, they would still be able to use it.
  c The Magna Carta was the beginning of Parliament. No king could rule without taking notice of what the barons wanted.
  d The Magna Carta was a 'turning-point' because it gave the barons something to build on in their struggle to make the king less powerful.

  e The Magna Carta was useless. The king was still in charge.

Which one of these statements do you think is *most* true? Explain why you think it is the most accurate statement.

❺ Now you have weighed up all the evidence, it is time to write an epitaph for King John. (This is a much shorter analysis of someone's life than the obituary you wrote for Thomas Becket: an epitaph is something that appears on a person's gravestone.) You will need to draw a gravestone in your book and try to sum up John's dealings with the barons in fewer than 25 words (or it won't fit on the gravestone) — but it *must* sum up John's problems and his solutions.

Here lies King John, a king remembered for...

Richard II versus the people (1381)

Throughout late June and July 1381 the roadsides of the southeast of England were littered with the rotting corpses of peasants that hung from makeshift gallows.

John Ball, a poor priest from York who had been forced out of his own parish by the arch-bishop, was hung, drawn and quartered on 15 July.

All these peasants had been killed on the orders of the king. What had gone *so wrong* that a king would want to seek revenge *so cruelly* on his own subjects?

To help you find out why the king was executing his own subjects it is necessary to look back at the events that had happened in June.

Wat Tyler and the rebels

On Friday 15 June the king, Richard II, rode out to Smithfield in London to meet the rebellious crowd and their leader, Wat Tyler, a peasant from Kent.

As the crowd looked on, Tyler rinsed his mouth with water and spat it out before the king. He played with a dagger, throwing it from hand to hand in a threatening manner. He made demands of the king and said that his men would not disperse until the demands had been met.

Activity

❶ You have to make a snap decision: was the king wrong or right to kill so many peasants?

To help you understand why the above events took place you are going to start to make a list of actions that the two different sides took. Copy the following table into your exercise book.

What the king's side did	What the peasants did
They executed a priest called John Ball.	

The king's reaction

The king was calm. He agreed to the demands on condition that the crowd dispersed. Tyler turned to remount his pony, when the Lord Mayor of London's valet shouted to him that his rudeness was shameful. Tyler turned and tried to stab the valet. William Walworth, the Lord Mayor, stopped Tyler, who tried to stab the Lord Mayor too.

The death of Tyler

The dagger did not pierce Walworth's armour, but the Mayor then drew his own dagger and stabbed Tyler in the neck. After that another of the king's men ran him through with his sword three times. Tyler was dead. The king rode up to the 20,000 rebels and told them that he was their king and that they should follow him. The rebels dispersed and went home.

Activity

❷ You can now add a little more detail to your table. Are you changing your mind about whether the king was right or wrong?

Wat Tyler is killed and Richard II tells the rebels to go home

The king and his advisers fled to the safety of the Tower of London

Key

— Route of rebels

ENGLAND

From Norfolk

From Suffolk

From Essex

London

From Kent

Map showing where the rebels came from

The rebels invade

Two days earlier, on 13 June, the news had swept through London that an enormous army was marching on the capital. It was a ragged army, but determined. The rebels came to London from a wide area, including Suffolk, Norfolk, Essex and Kent.

This was no foreign invasion; it was welcomed by the poor of London, who offered food and water to the rebels. Some say this army numbered 100,000.

The rebels began burning the houses of the king's advisers. Then they set about finding lawyers to set fire to their houses too. They burnt down the Temple, where all legal records were stored.

What happened next?

The king and his advisers fled to the safety of William the

Conqueror's White Tower (the Tower of London), the safest refuge in the capital. They watched in fear as the city was overrun by drunken rebels. The Fleet prison was ransacked and its prisoners set free. The palace of John O'Gaunt, the king's uncle, was burnt down.

Worse was to come. The rebels controlled the city. They surrounded the Tower of London and demanded to see the king.

The meeting at Mile End

Richard met the rebels at Mile End on the following day. Their demands were clear (see **Source A**).

The outcome

The terrified King Richard II, facing the desperate mob, agreed to the rebels' demands. He then told them to go home. But some still wanted more.

The rebels broke into the Tower and dragged the king's chief adviser, Simon Sudbury (the Archbishop of Canterbury), and Roger Hales (the Treasurer of England) out into the street and hacked off their heads; it took eight blows to sever Sudbury's. His mitre was then nailed to his head, before both men's heads were stuck on poles and displayed on London Bridge for all to see.

Source A

The rebels' demands

✤ All 'traitors' should be handed over to them.

✤ Serfdom (slavery) should be abolished.

✤ All peasants should receive fair wages and cheaper rents.

✤ All who had taken part in the revolt should be pardoned.

Activity

❶ Having read the above account, now add more detail to your table.

❷ What are the links between the actions of the king and the actions of the peasants?

❸ Have you changed your opinion about the king or the peasants? If so, in what way?

❹ If this were a film, what might its title be?

❺ Design a poster to advertise the film. To help you, look at the poster below. Examine the way it has been drawn and the way it tries to show the exciting aspects of the film. What details do you think should be included in your poster to sum up the events described above?

A film poster

The Peasants' Revolt

You have just read about the end of an event known as the Peasants' Revolt. You have probably spotted some links between what the king did and what the peasants did. The actions of both sides were influenced by what the other side did. In the next task you will be looking for some more reasons why each side acted as it did.

10 Labourers were freer than ever before — they were less dependent on their lords — and they became much bolder.

9 The peasants felt that a violent protest would help them persuade the king to give in to their demands.

Richard II

1 John Ball, a priest, started spreading ideas about everyone being equal.

2 Taxes continued to rise. Between 1377 and 1381 the charge trebled.

8 The government had failed to control the wages of labourers in 1351 when lords ignored the Statute of Labourers.

3 The king often imposed a poll tax in order to raise funds.

7 Richard II was only 10 years old when he became king.

4 England was constantly at war with France at this time and was clearly losing.

5 There was unrest in various parts of England, especially in Norfolk, Suffolk, Essex and Kent.

6 The Black Death of 1348 killed off many labourers.

A

The shortage of farm labourers meant that the lords had to pay more money to get workers.

B

The peasants began to react by murdering the tax collectors.

C

Taxes continued to rise to pay for the wars against France.

D

The peasants believed that they should have the same rights as everyone else.

E

King Richard II had to rely on advisers who did not always give the best guidance.

F

The king was terrified but decided that a strong response was required.

G

Labourers were able to get improved wages and in 1368 in some places they were allowed to rent land from the lords.

H

Poll taxes were levied on all: everyone paid the same charge whether they were rich or poor.

I

Some labourers were becoming richer and did not have to do 3 days of unpaid work for their lord.

J

The peasants were disorganised, but a leader eventually emerged — Wat Tyler.

Activity

❷ Now look at all the causes again. Which ones are **long-term** causes of the Peasants' Revolt (things that had begun to happen beforehand and carried on)? Which ones are **short-term** causes (things that were closer to the event and were more of a spark)?

❸ Which of the causes was the *most* important in bringing about the Peasants' Revolt?

❹ Which one of the cause–effect pairs was not really a cause of the revolt, but more of a cause and effect *during* the revolt?

❺ If you were making a Venn diagram to show these causes, which three categories would you use? Draw a Venn diagram in your exercise book and place the causes in the correct places.

❻ Do you think there was anything that the king or his advisers could have done to avoid the Peasants' Revolt?

❼ Were the peasants right to threaten the king the way they did? What sort of tactics do people use today when they want to campaign for change? How different are these tactics from the Peasants' Revolt of 1381?

❽ Do you think there might have been any long-term consequences for the king and the peasants as a result of this event?

❾ The following question requires you to make a decision that you will have to back up with facts. The more points you can make with examples to support them, the stronger your argument will be:

Who was to blame for the Peasants' Revolt?

Who lost most power in medieval England?

Topic 3 has concentrated on the clashes between the monarchy and the Church, the barons and the people, over a period of just over 200 years.

Henry II He faced a serious challenge to his reign in the shape of religion. The murder of Becket not only led to a falling out of the Church and the monarchy, but also made Henry look cruel and ruthless.

John The barons' revolt was a threat to the power of the monarch because the feudal system depended on their loyalty. Now they had turned against the crown it would be difficult for future kings to trust the nobles.

Richard II His harsh punishment of the rebels meant that the king lost the trust of the peasants. There was little hope for the feudal system after this. The peasants would have to find other ways of challenging the king.

Activity

Read the statements below and decide which ones are true and which are false. If you think a statement is true, write it down and **give a reason** to back up your answer. If it is false you need to **change** the statement to **make it true**. For example:

'The peasants were a bigger threat to the monarchy and its power than the Church or the barons.'

False. There were a lot of peasants, and they definitely scared the monarchy when they rebelled, but they were easily beaten. Richard II told them to go home on 14 June 1381, and most of them did. The rest were hunted down and hanged in the months following the revolt.

So the statement should read: *'The peasants were a big threat to the monarchy when they rebelled, but they were easily controlled in the end.'*

1   The monarchy faced the biggest challenge to its power from the Church, as the Church was constantly trying to chip away at the king's authority.

2   The monarchy remained the strongest power in the land throughout the period.

3   The barons benefited most by the loss of the monarchy's authority.

4   The monarchy used the nobles to keep a grip on its power.

5   The monarchy always used violence and threats to maintain its authority.

6   The ordinary people were constantly trying to chip away at the monarchy's authority.

7   The monarchy was losing its power throughout this period.

8   The monarchy had lost a lot of its power to the nobles, as they had a say in how the country should be run by 1381.

9   The king was still the most powerful person in the country by 1381.

10 The monarchy made sure that there would be no problems in the future by controlling the Church and the nobles, and quelling the rebellion by the peasants.

Norman castles

After William's victory at Hastings he was crowned King of England, and yet we know him as the Conqueror. But he faced a long, hard task if he was to gain control and conquer England.

He decided very quickly that building castles was the best way to do this. They were built throughout England, to serve as bases for Norman knights. Castles were places of safety where knights could take refuge if they were attacked. They could also use them as stores or just as places to take rest.

Motte and bailey castles

The first motte and bailey castles were built rapidly; they consisted of a wooden keep on a huge mound of earth surrounded by a wooden fence called a palisade (see page 14). But these were only a temporary measure. The Normans knew that these castles had weaknesses.

Stone castles

By about 1100 the castles were built out of stone. They still had a keep and it was usually square, like the one shown here. They became less cramped and less uncomfortable to live in, although there were still some problems.

A Norman keep

Life in a medieval castle 1

With the right defences a castle could be an impregnable fortress, but it could also be just an impressive home. Life inside a castle was busy and bustling; it was the home of an entire community looking after a rich noble and his family. For some nobles their castles gave them a chance to show just how important, powerful and wealthy they were. You are going to use the artist's recontruction opposite to look at the way people had to live in castles.

Activity

❶ Look carefully at the picture of the castle. Try to find the following things:
  a a tapestry — an embroidered picture hung on a wall
  b a cresset — a torch that was usually hung on a wall
  c a well — the water supply
  d a garderobe — a structure that hung over the castle walls, so that when people went to the toilet it dropped straight outside
  e a spit — a device that was used to roast meat over an open fire; a dripping tray underneath caught all the juices
  f an armoury — where all the weapons were kept
  g the basement — where all the foodstuffs and wine were kept
  h a dog — the medieval waste disposal unit
  i a chapel — for religious services

❷ Look at the list of items in the castle again.
  a What do these features tell us about the way people lived?
  b How does their life compare with the way we live today?
  c Choose **three** features from this castle that you think are good and another **three** features that are not so pleasant. Explain your choice after each one.

❸ Look at the four scenes marked A–D. Choose one of them and write a paragraph as if you were the main person in the picture, to explain what aspect of castle life it shows and why it is important to life in the castle.

Thinking aloud

What weaknesses might a wooden castle have?

What difficulties might you find in building a castle out of stone?

Life in a medieval castle 2

Starter activity

Think about how different the life of a noble would have been from that of a servant in a castle. Look at the graph below. It depicts the experiences of a servant shown as a **fortune line**, or how he might have felt at different times during the day. Statements **a** to **l** include some of the servant's experiences throughout the day and some of his master's. You have to work out which are which.

❶ Copy the graph into your exercise book.

❷ Write on the letters from the servant's day in the places where you think they should go.

❸ Draw the noble's fortune line to show his experiences and label the line with the letters in the places you think they fit best.

a 7.00 p.m. The wines have been selected and I am about to serve at the feast. I am very nervous. I don't want anything to go wrong.

b 9.00 a.m. I will see my chaplain for his daily blessing, before I speak to my trusted knights.

c 2.00 p.m. After seeing off the hunting party my work will begin on preparing the feast for their return. This will involve standing and turning the whole lamb on the roasting spit in front of a roaring fire for up to 3 hours.

d 5.00 a.m. I have to be up early to make sure that the fire in the kitchen is lit. It is very cold.

e 11.30 p.m. The minstrels have kept me entertained all evening with their witty songs and their tales of old knights on quests, and now I am ready to sleep.

f 6.00 p.m. I will require someone to help me dress after my hunting trip.

g 10.30 a.m. My Lord's horse will be needed for the hunt this afternoon. I will have to groom the horses and prepare the saddles for the whole party.

h Midnight. I am still clearing away the pots and pans, but I will get to my bed of straw soon. I am exhausted, but I am lucky to live here with a kind master.

i 10.00 a.m. There are many duties to perform, such as raising fresh water from the well.

j 9.30 p.m. My banquets are always successful. I am keen to feed my knights well. They protect me.

k 1.00 p.m. I will take my luncheon with mead and snooze peacefully for an hour before I ride the hunt.

l 7.30 a.m. I rise from my bed and eat cold meats for breakfast.

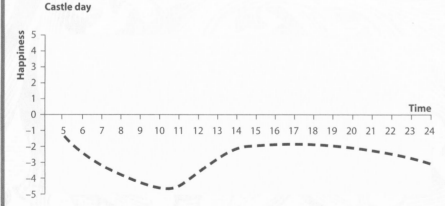

Castle day

The reliability of sources

Historians need to question the sources of information they have to help them build a picture of the past. Some sources are more reliable than others. Reliability of a source can depend on factors such as how long after the event it was recorded, who produced it and why it was produced.

Sources A and **B** were taken from *The Once and Future King* by T. H. White (1939), the book used to create the well-known Disney cartoon *The Sword in the Stone*. Read the sources and then complete activities 1 to 3.

Source A

The Wart got up early next morning. He made a determined effort the moment he woke, threw off the great bearskin rug under which he slept, and plunged his body into the biting air. He dressed furiously, trembling, skipping about to keep warm, and hissing blue breaths to himself as if he were grooming a horse. He broke the ice in the basin and dipped his face in it with a grimace like eating something sour, said A-a-a-ah, and rubbed his stinging cheeks vigorously with a towel.

Adapted from White, T. H. (1939) *The Once and Future King*

Source B

Sir Ector sat in the solar, while the wintering sunlight threw broad orange beams across his bald head. He scratched and spluttered away, and laboriously bit the end of his pen, and the castle room darkened about him. It was a room as big as the main hall over which it stood, and it could afford to have large southern windows because it was on the second storey. There were two fireplaces, in which the ashy logs of wood turned from grey to red as the sunlight retreated. Round these, some favourite hounds lay snuffling in their dreams, or scratching themselves for fleas, or gnawing mutton bones which they had scrounged from the kitchens. The peregrine falcon stood hooded on a perch in the corner, a motionless idol dreaming of other skies.

Adapted from White, T. H. (1939) *The Once and Future King*

Activity

❶ What do **Sources A** and **B** tell us about the different kinds of lives people led in a medieval castle?

❷ How many of the details could the author have known as fact?

❸ How reliable are these extracts as a source of information?

❹ Make a mind movie: close your eyes and try to imagine yourself in any room in a medieval castle where people might have lived. You have 30 seconds in which to try to think of all the things you can see.

❺ Quickly write a list of what you saw.

❻ Find a partner and compare your lists. Between you, work out five things that you think could only really exist in a medieval castle room.

❼ Where do you think you got your mental images from? How reliable are they?

How were castles defended?

Castles were, first and foremost, defensive fortresses. Medieval castle designers faced a great challenge in devising ever more secure buildings. They learned a lot from the Muslim castle builders during the Crusades of the twelfth century.

One major improvement concerned the walls. Instead of just one they built a series of walls, one inside the other, with each higher than the one in front. These **concentric** castles also had a much better fortified gatehouse, with two enormous rounded towers at each side of the gate. This type of gatehouse was called the **barbican**.

Inside the walls was the infamous 'killing ground', where two **portcullises** could be used to trap an army while archers fired arrows down from above. There were many other fiendish ways of defending the castle, as the diagrams here show.

A **parapet** ran along the tops of the walls, so that men could fight from them. To give them extra cover the walls had **crenellations** (extra bits of wall).

The simplest way to strengthen the defences of a castle was to flood the **moat**.

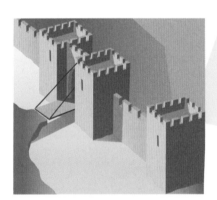

The rounded towers had **arrow slits** in the shape of a cross so that crossbows and longbows could be used in them.

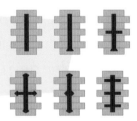

The barbican also had a very sneaky defence: in the arches of the outside wall it had **drop holes** where soldiers could drop stones or boiling water on the enemy below.

A **rounded tower** was built at every corner. This was an easy way to keep an eye on the walls and also to get rid of corners, which were easy to chip away at in an attack.

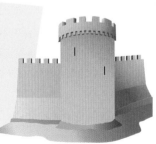

The **walls** of castles got thicker and thicker. Some were 2 metres thick around the barbican. The walls got thicker towards the bottom too. This was so stones that were dropped would bounce away towards the enemy.

Caerphilly castle

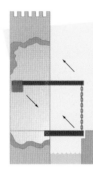

The barbican housed the **drawbridge**, a safety feature that allowed the defenders to pull up the bridge to stop people crossing the moat.

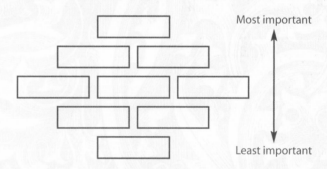

The front and rear of the barbican also housed the **portcullis** (French for a criss-crossed door). The heavy wooden gates had metal spikes at the bottom. They could be raised and dropped very quickly.

A **well** was a defensive feature that had to be thought of early in the castle-building plan. It would save lives during a siege. The castle on page 35 had a deep well in the basement.

Activity

❶ Look at the nine features opposite. All of them were of some help in defending a castle, but which do you think were likely to be the most effective?

❷ Copy the following diagram into your exercise book.

Most important

Least important

❸ In pairs, decide which features would be most important in helping to defend a castle. Put what you consider to be the most important feature at the top and the least important feature at the bottom.

❹ When you are certain of your order, write the names of the features in the boxes. Make sure that you can justify your choices to your partner.

❺ Look at the modern-day photograph of the remains of Caerphilly castle. How many of the defences listed opposite can you see?

Numeracy and ICT exercises

Historians have to interpret many different types of **secondary source**. These can be as diverse as letters to friends, church accounts and paintings. Making sense of the information and seeing how it links to other sources is a key part of historical interpretation.

Castle building: do the sums add up?

Some figures about castle building are displayed as a scatter graph in **Source A**. The graph plots two variables about castle building, but what does it tell us?

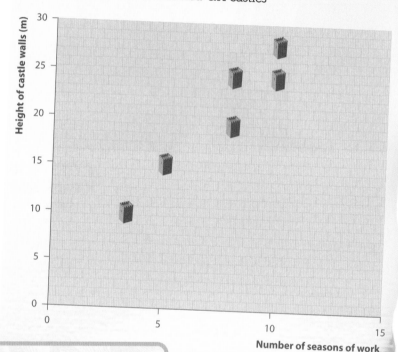

Source A

The height of castle walls in relation to the time taken to build them for selected UK castles

Height of castle walls (m) (y-axis: 0, 5, 10, 15, 20, 25, 30)

Number of seasons of work (x-axis: 0, 5, 10, 15)

Numeracy activity

❶ Say which of the following statements is true and which is false. You will need at least one piece of evidence to back up each answer.
  a Castles with high walls were quick to build.
  b The longer it took to build a castle, the higher it became.
  c The higher the walls, the longer the castle took to build.
  d There is a negative correlation between how long it took a castle to be built and how high the walls were.
  e Castles that took the same amount of time to build were the same height.
  f There is a positive correlation between how long castles took to build and their height.
  g We can predict from the graph how long it might have taken to build a castle with 30-metre walls.
  h On average it took about two seasons of work to add 6 metres to the height of a castle.

Numeracy activity

2 What effect do you think the following factors would have had on the time it took to build a castle? Explain your reasons.

a Poor-quality local stone
b The start of a major war
c The wealth of the baron
d Friendship with the king
e A remote location

3 Look at **Source B**. Today the average cost of a house is around £200,000 and the average wage is about £20,000. How and why would the following extra sources of information help us make sense of the figures in the table?

a The size of each castle
b The date it was finished
c The average wage in Britain in medieval times

ICT activity

Historians need to know how to use the vast amount of secondary source information available. One way of keeping, sorting and filtering information is to use a spreadsheet.

1 Enter the data from **Source C** into a new spreadsheet page.

2 Highlight the header row (so that Row 1 is dark) by placing the arrow to the left of the row and clicking the right mouse button.

3 Then click on the **Data** option at the top of the page and select **AutoFilter** from the drop-down menu. The column names will now be ready to filter and they will have a small black arrow by the side of each heading name (e.g. **Date**).

4 Click on the **Date** arrow and from the drop-down list choose (**Custom**...). From the pop-up dialogue box, choose the option 'show rows where Date is: *less than – 1100'*.

5 The list will now hide all castles except those that were built before 1100. What do you notice about the location of these castles?

6 Repeat the exercise with the **Date** filter, but this time choose (**All**...) to reset, then find out where the castles built after 1280 are located. Suggest reasons for any differences in location. (Hint: where did the conquest of Wales begin from?)

Source C

Castle data for spreadsheet

Name	Date	County	Region	Type
Beaumaris	1295	Anglesey	NW	Coastal
Caernarfon	1283	Gwynedd	NW	Coastal
Caerphilly	1267	Caerphilly	S	Routeway
Cardiff	1081	Cardiff	S	Coastal
Carmarthen	1116	Carmarthen	W	Coastal
Carreg Cennen	1190	Carmarthen	SW	Routeway
Chepstow	1067	Monmouth	SE	Coastal
Clyro	1070	Powys	E	Border
Conwy	1283	Conwy	NW	Coastal
Denbigh	1282	Denbigh	NE	Border
Flint	1277	Flintshire	NE	Coastal
Grosmont	1138	Monmouth	E	Border
Harlech	1283	Gwynedd	NW	Coastal
Kenfig	1185	Bridgend	SW	Coastal
Kidwelly	1114	Carmarthen	SW	Coastal
Laugharne	1116	Carmarthen	SW	Coastal
Llandovery	1116	Carmarthen	SW	Routeway
Llansteffan	1146	Carmarthen	SW	Coastal
Monmouth	1071	Monmouth	SE	Border
Powis	1110	Powys	NE	Border

Source B

The cost of castles in Wales

Castle	Cost in £ (medieval)
Aberystwyth	3,885
Beaumaris	14,444
Builth	1,666
Caernarfon	19,892
Conwy	14,248
Flint	8,951
Harlech	6,244
Average	9,904

Why did castle defences change?

Walking around a ruined castle today, it is hard to imagine how castles dominated life in this country for so much of the Middle Ages. They changed through time from strongholds to the grandest houses, from wooden structures to fortresses of stone, from early Norman keeps to late Tudor gun batteries. Their changing shape and size reflects their changing purpose as they responded to advances in technology.

You have read a lot about castles in this topic. The following activity will allow you to assess how much you have learned.

Activity

Form and function

It is the 1150s and you are the chief stonemason for a Norman castle that is about to undergo some changes. The baron has told you that you are responsible for the redevelopment of the castle to make it safer from attack. He can only afford three of the eight possible alterations shown in **Source B** and, ideally, he needs them within 5 years.

To help you decide, look at the diagrams and building times of the alterations (**Source B**), and also at the extract from the letter (**Source A**). This is part of a letter from the baron to the king asking for funds and expressing his concerns.

❶ Study **Sources A** and **B**. Choose the three alterations from **Source B** that you think would best help the baron to solve his problems.

❷ Write a report for the baron to help him decide how best to defend his castle in the time available.

❸ Explain in which order the alterations should be built.

❹ For each choice, explain why it would help him to defend his castle.

Skill box

PEEL away the layers of historical evidence to find the gem of an answer. You may have many interesting things to say in your answer but the most important thing is to select the right evidence to back up your argument.

Make a **P**oint, give some **E**vidence to support it, **E**xplain what you mean, then **L**ink your points together.

For example:

One important extra feature the castle needs is a tower (**P**). This is a tall stone building, with a staircase, that might be built above the main keep to provide a lookout position (**E**). This would mean there would be far less chance of being surprised by an attack (**E**). If this form of early warning was linked to another feature such as a portcullis (**L**),…

Source A

…There have been many attacks on nearby castles in recent months and I fear it cannot be long before our defences are tried and found wanting. We are so low down by the river that we are overlooked by hills on all sides and are unable to see the enemy until they are upon us. Kempley and Durstang were both besieged last year for over 3 months and nearly fell. The enemy have used siege towers and mined under their walls. The building stone here is poor but if your grace could grant us funds we could add the new-style defences that could help us make this area safe and keep the road west open.…

Part of a letter from the baron to the king

Source B

Possible alterations and their building times

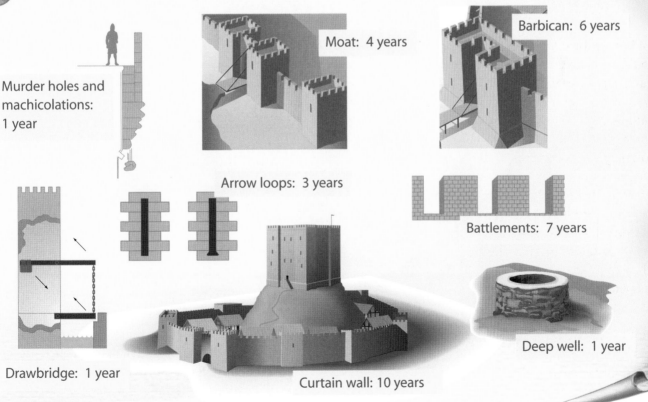

Murder holes and machicolations: 1 year

Moat: 4 years

Barbican: 6 years

Arrow loops: 3 years

Battlements: 7 years

Drawbridge: 1 year

Curtain wall: 10 years

Deep well: 1 year

Was it a better life in the countryside?

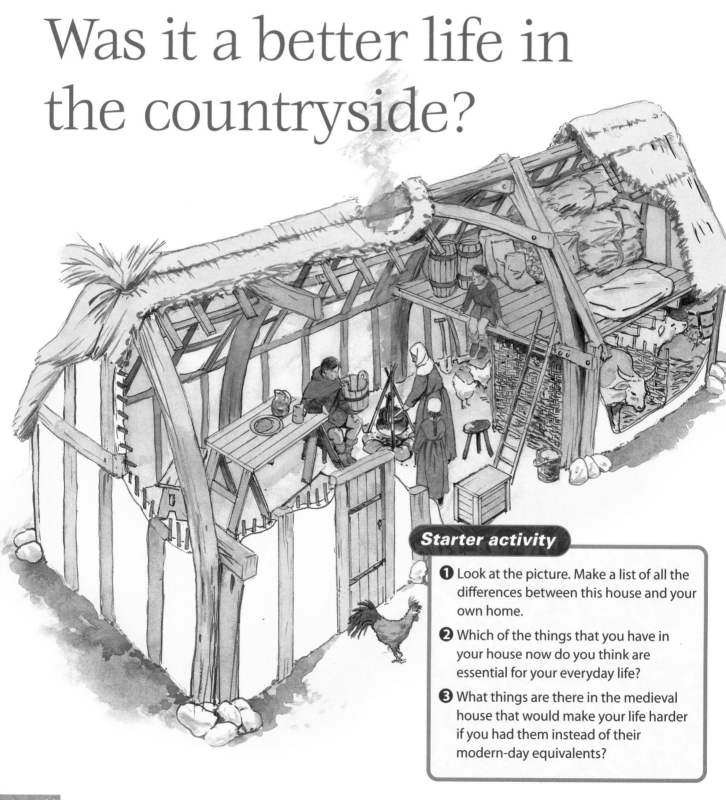

Starter activity

❶ Look at the picture. Make a list of all the differences between this house and your own home.

❷ Which of the things that you have in your house now do you think are essential for your everyday life?

❸ What things are there in the medieval house that would make your life harder if you had them instead of their modern-day equivalents?

You are going to make a comparison between the lives of two ordinary people during medieval times. One will be a **villein** who lived in the countryside and the other will be a town dweller.

Villeins lived and worked on the lord of the manor's land. They got their houses in return for working the land.

The villein's house

Looking at this artist's impression of a villein's house, it is easy to see that a villein's life would be hard. But there are some other facts that you need to know about to be able to make a more informed judgement about the life of a villein.

Building materials
The walls were made of **wattle and daub** — a woven panel of wooden branches, known as a hurdle, covered over with clay (and dung to help it set harder).

The roof was **thatched** — bunched reeds that covered a timber frame. Glass was expensive so most houses had few windows.

Inside the house
Light came from rushes dipped in animal fat — a bit like a candle, but not as bright. On the earth floor there were usually rushes scattered about to make it a little warmer, and also to catch any animal droppings as the animals shared the room too.

Who did the work?
To keep down the cost of building, most people did as much as possible of the building work themselves. Some jobs, however, like the thatching and the hurdling, were quite skilled. Some of the skilled craftsmen who did this work tended to travel around their area, as they were in demand. The materials that they used often depended on what they found nearby where they were working.

Source A

John Raynauld broke into and entered at night the Lord's park where he took 17 oak trees which he used to repair his house.

John Shephard is fined because the clay he took to place on the outside of his walls of his house was taken from the common roadway.

John Yude wants to lease one of the rooms in his house to someone else for a period of one year.

It is ordered that no one must go into the area known as Le Holme and take rushes to place on their roof or their floor.

Four villagers have been fined for carrying away the door of a waste house. This consisted of the wood, a socket stone, iron hanging post, a key, padlock, hinges and a latch.

Alice Kaa broke down the doors and windows and took away lamps and oil.

Philip Hogyns must repair the kitchen in his building.

Extract from a manorial court record

Activity
❶ What do you notice about all the materials that were required to build a villein's house?

❷ Look at the extract from a manorial court record (**Source A**). What difficulties were there for a villein building a house on the lord's manor?

The life of a villein

Villeins had few possessions, as you could see in the picture on page 44.

What did villeins own?

A table and benches were vital, as were storage items like wooden barrels and tubs, bowls, cups, ladles and spoons. They had knives and cooking pots, which were made of metal.

Some people had a mattress made of linen stuffed with straw, which made sleeping on the floor more comfortable. They owned few clothes, so a wardrobe was unnecessary.

What did villeins live on?

Working the land was their primary job, but after working in the lord of the manor's fields any spare time could be spent cultivating their own small patch of land around their house. Fruit trees, such as apple and pear, were common.

Many kept bees for honey, which was used to sweeten food or to preserve fruits. Vegetables like carrots, leeks, onions and cabbage were staple foods.

Cows, pigs and chickens were vital to survival. When they had been slaughtered they were preserved by being salted or smoked. Oxen were kept for ploughing the lord's fields.

If the crops failed there was little to fall back on, other than wild rabbits or fish from the rivers. The threat of starvation was never far away.

The grinding of wheat to make flour and the baking of bread had to be done in the lord's mill and ovens, and the villeins had to pay for the privilege. The lord had the first pick of the loaves and usually chose the unburnt bread at the top of the oven. (This is why richer people are sometimes referred to today as the upper crust.)

Using oxen to plough the lord's fields

1. Make a list of all the things a villein had to pay for or do as payment to the lord.

2. Design an advert to sell the villein's house on page 44. As a good estate agent you will need to point out the good features of the house, but you should also try to put the best spin that you can on its not-so-pleasant aspects. Try to think of ways of explaining all the features of the house, good and bad, in a positive way. You will also have to tell prospective buyers what they will have to do to get the house. Remember to tell them about the villein's duties.

3. Nowadays we expect our houses to have hot and cold running water, electricity, a toilet, bathroom and kitchen. The medieval villein had none of these. For each one of these amenities, write down what you think the villeins did/used instead.

4. If you were a modern-day health inspector visiting the villein's house, what would be your top **ten** health concerns? Compile a numbered list.

5. Thinking about all the information that you know about the lifestyle of the villein, which of the following statements do you agree with most? Explain your choice.

   a. Villeins had to work very hard all year round if they were to survive, but at least the environment that they lived in was healthy.

   b. Life in the countryside was a constant struggle and villeins had to be skilled in a number of things just to get by.

Everyone had to do the back-breaking work of reaping the lord's wheat

Taxes

Villeins also had to pay taxes. The types of tax demanded included: free food whenever the lord demanded it and a tax (called a **merchet**) when the daughter of a villein wanted to marry. Villeins even had to pay taxes on their death: a **mortuary** was paid to the Church, and all the villein's possessions were given to the lord of the manor. Widows were left with nothing.

Why didn't villeins run away?

They could not leave without the permission of the lord. They were tied to him and his land. Without the lord they had nothing.

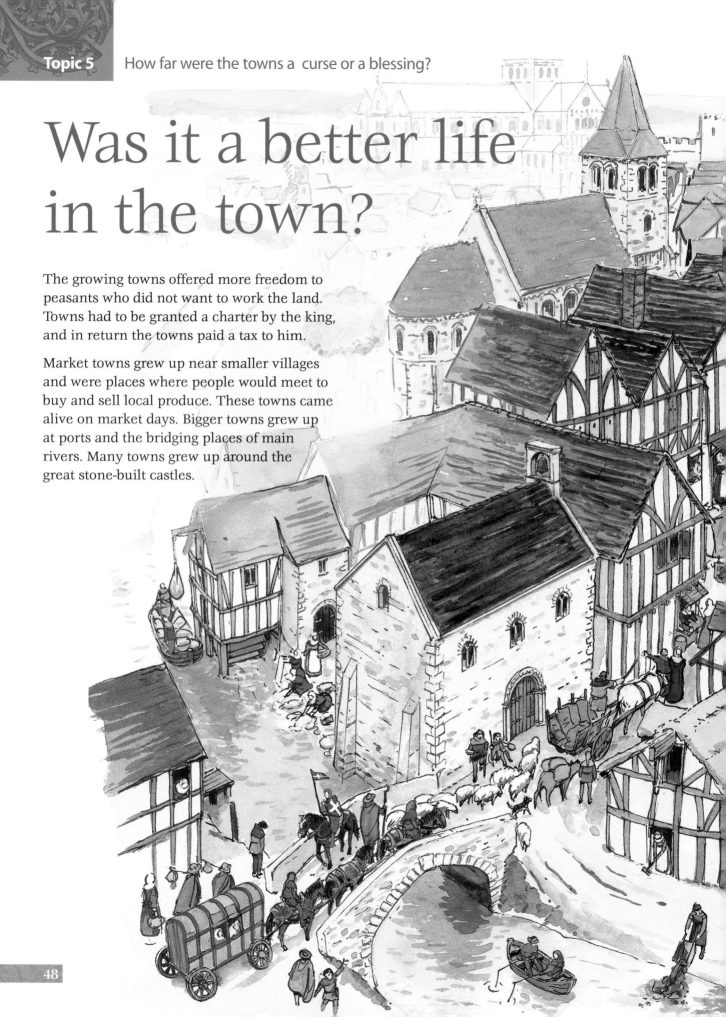

Was it a better life in the town?

The growing towns offered more freedom to peasants who did not want to work the land. Towns had to be granted a charter by the king, and in return the towns paid a tax to him.

Market towns grew up near smaller villages and were places where people would meet to buy and sell local produce. These towns came alive on market days. Bigger towns grew up at ports and the bridging places of main rivers. Many towns grew up around the great stone-built castles.

This picture shows a typical medieval town. Imagine you are a town dweller in medieval times and take a walk through the town. Study the picture closely and point out all the sights you can see. You should also think carefully about the sorts of things you might hear and the smells that would be around. As you read out your description of your trail through the town, everyone else in the room should be able to follow it. Your description should give them all the information they need.

How easy was it to live in a town?

Perhaps the most striking thing about the medieval town was the fact that the streets and houses were so close together (see the photograph of the Shambles in York). There were no cars to worry about, so the streets tended to be full of people. As you can see from the picture on pages 48–49, animals wandered freely, rummaging through the rubbish and waste that people hurled out of their windows.

When people heard the shout 'gardey loo!' from a window above, they stepped out of the way. (The expression comes from the French '*gardez l'eau*', meaning 'watch out for the water' — it's why we say we go to the 'loo' today.)

Shops

There were no windows in shops, and shutters folded down to form a counter, so shop-keepers sold their goods from a stall at the front of their shops. There were streets of shops all selling the same goods. People were free to handle and examine the goods on sale before they bought them.

Freemen

It seemed that people who lived in towns could do as they pleased. So how did you become a town dweller?

In the early thirteenth century some towns had a royal charter stating that if a villein who had run away from his master could live in the town and support himself and pay his taxes for a year and a day, he would be a **freeman**.

Town guilds

With so many people making and selling goods there had to be some way of controlling what went on.

Look at the closeness of the houses and shops in this medieval street, the Shambles, in modern-day York

Activity

❶ You are going to begin your comparison with life in the countryside. If you were a modern-day health inspector visiting the town on pages 48–49, what would be your top **ten** health concerns? Compile a numbered list.

❷ Look back at your list for the villein's house. Are any of your concerns about it similar to the ones you have just listed for the town?

❸ Are any of your concerns different, or are they specifically to do with living in the town?

Each craft or trade set up a town guild, the purpose of which was to check the quality of goods on sale. These town guilds were a way of making sure that only the best-quality goods were sold at a fair price. The guilds also regulated how things were made (see **Source A**).

Not only did the guilds control how good the work was, they also specified the prices that people could charge.

Master craftsmen

To become a craftsman a person had to spend 7 years learning the craft as an **apprentice**. After their work was checked, by the guild, they could become a **journeyman** for another 7 years before they produced their 'masterpiece', which allowed them to become a **master craftsman**.

Protecting local traders

The town guilds were keen to enforce their standards and they were prepared to protect their members. Town officials also protected townsmen by making any traders who came from other places, like market stallholders, pay a toll to get into the town and also a tax for each good they sold. This meant that traders from outside were paying a lot more than local people for the right to trade in the town. It also helped raise the funds to pay the taxes owed to the king for granting the town a charter in the first place.

Source A

Strict rules were used to govern how goods were produced in towns

No outside traders can sell cloth within the town.

No member of the Guild can take more than one apprentice at a time.

The widow of a member can continue the trade until the stock runs out, but not longer than three months.

Adapted from Shephard, C. et al. (1991)
Discovering the Past: Contrasts and Connections

Town councils

It was not long before the town officials became even more important: they formed town councils and their rules began to extend even further than just dealing with trades. They set about making their town safer, cleaner and better for traders and merchants to visit.

Activity

The guildsmen were very powerful people, but who were their rules designed to protect? Look at **Source A**.

❹ Copy out each of the guild rules listed in **Source A** and alongside each one write down who would benefit from it. Be careful because sometimes more than one person or group might benefit.

❺ The following guild rules were taken from a few different towns. If you were a locksmith, which of these rules would you use?
   a No one is allowed to work when the sun goes down.
   b Banging and hammering is not permitted in the hours of darkness.
   c No spare keys are to be sold in the town.
   d All locks must be made in the same way.
   e All locksmiths in the town should carry a master key.

❻ Explain why you would use the rules that you have chosen.

❼ Can you think of any alternative rules that you might use as a locksmith?

❽ Explain who the rules might benefit.

Who had the better life: townsfolk or countryfolk?

The different lifestyles experienced by town and village dwellers can be seen clearly in the concerns listed on these pages.

Remember that a town had to have a charter from the king to exist. The townsfolk paid taxes so that the charter could be kept. Just like villeins, there were costs to pay, but a town dweller was a freeman as long as he could pay his way.

As you read through the statements below, think about who had the best life. Who was most secure? Who was the most free? What dangers faced people living in the town and in the country?

Activity

The statements in the bubbles were made by the five people pictured here. They were talking about their lives in medieval times. All you have to do is to decide which people said what. Think about what you know about life in the towns and life in the country.

f Some towns make more of an effort to welcome me, so I don't mind paying their tolls.

a I could lose my home at any time.

b When I die my wife will probably be poor, unless she can find work in the town.

d I face heavy fines if I don't do as I am instructed.

c I know that whatever I buy inside the town walls will be of a good standard.

e I could be put out of business very easily.

Villein

Guild master

g We don't want too many people in business as we want to keep the prices high.

j My family and I are safe in our house as long as we work hard enough to bring in the crops.

k I'm responsible for making sure that everyone gets to buy the same standard of goods while they are in this town.

h When I die my wife could be homeless and she will lose everything we have.

l I'm free to do whatever I want in the town now that I have lived here for a year and a day.

Freeman

i My payments to the lord make it very difficult for us to get by sometimes.

m It's very difficult getting my goods into town, as I have to pay a toll at the gate, or set out my stall by the town walls.

n I can't make as much money as I want to because the rules are so strict.

Craftsman

o I would love to get away from the controls that I am continually under.

Travelling merchant

p I have had to train for 14 years to get to where I am. One mistake could ruin my business.

Overview activity

❶ What were the advantages and disadvantages of being a villein?

❷ What were the advantages and disadvantages of being a freeman?

❸ If you had to choose to be either a townsman or a villein, which would you choose? Explain your answer clearly.

Were medieval doctors effective?

Starter activity

How many different people do we need to help us to get better today? Make a list of as many healthcare workers as you can.

When we are ill we want to be cured quickly, and usually we don't care how we get cured as long as it works. People in medieval times were exactly the same, but they only lived for about 40–50 years on average, not for nearly 80 as we do today.

People lived far harder lives than we do today and small illnesses from which we recover easily were life-threatening to them. In short, they were closer to death and expected illness to end their lives. They had faith in their medical experts, though, as we do today.

Characteristics that might be found in a doctor

- Knows where and how to cut open veins
- Wears a clean white coat
- Has clean hands
- Is a sympathetic listener
- Is young
- Has good eyesight
- Is male
- Can speak Latin
- Is old
- Is well educated
- Is religious
- Has medical training
- Has up-to-date technology and instruments
- Has a long list of living patients
- Makes up his/her own cures
- Is able to stop bleeding
- Has a collection of old medical books
- Dresses in expensive clothes
- Understands about the functions of the main organs
- Has seen the inside of a human body
- Has his/her own herb garden
- Has a good knowledge of music
- Knows the names of the main organs of the body
- Has seen the inside of an animal's body
- Is able to draw a skeleton

Activity

❶ Look at the list of characteristics that might be found in a doctor (**Source A**).

With a partner, choose **ten** qualities that you would look for if you were seeking someone to give good medical advice. Be prepared to justify your choices.

❷ In medieval times a medical professional might not have had all the qualities that you have listed. If you had to cut your list down to **five** essentials, what would they be? Be prepared to give **reasons** for your decisions.

A good medieval doctor

In the Middle Ages doctors were expected to be well educated and to be able to explain things clearly. People expected them to have studied the medical knowledge from years ago, and as this was in Latin and Greek, doctors were expected to understand these languages too.

Doctors should also like music as it was believed that it had **therapeutic** qualities.

A medieval examination

A doctor's examination of a patient might have run something like this:

- The doctor would visit his patient and ask how long she had felt unwell.
- He would use his good mathematical skills to calculate the patient's pulse.
- The next step might be to compare the patient's urine sample against a urine chart that the doctor would be expected to carry (see picture). The chart would usually be found in the doctor's **vade-mecum** (a little book containing information about a wide range of medical problems). The colour of the urine might indicate the internal health of the patient. The clearer a person's urine sample was, the healthier they were.

- But no good doctor would try to make a diagnosis yet. One of the most important considerations for a medieval doctor was to be able to cast his patient's **horoscope**, before suggesting a cure for the illness.

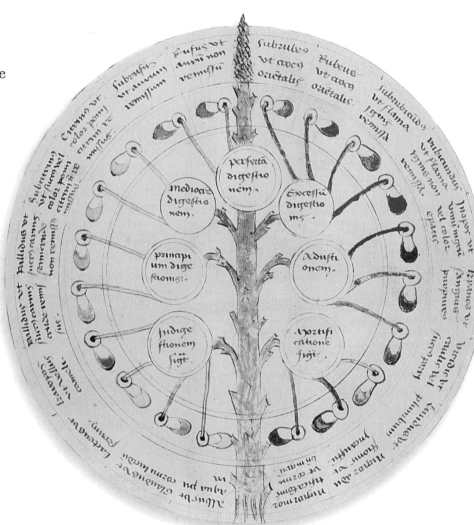

A doctor would use this urine chart to tell how well a patient was

Fact box

The theory of the four humours

Medieval doctors believed that the elements making up a person's body could become out of balance, which would make the person ill. This was linked to different times of the year, for example too much 'fire' in summer would make you sweat.

Humour	Temper	Organ	Nature	Element
Black bile	Melancholic	Spleen	Cold dry	Earth
Phlegm	Phlegmatic	Lungs	Cold wet	Water
Blood	Sanguine	Head	Warm wet	Air
Yellow bile	Choleric	Gall bladder	Warm dry	Fire

Zodiac man

Activity

❶ Study the picture of Zodiac man. Try to name all the birth signs and match them up to the parts of the body to which they refer. Can you work out what sorts of disorders you might suffer from if you were an Aquarian, a Leo, a Sagittarian?

❷ It is now time to make your first decision about the effectiveness of medieval doctors. Copy the line below into your exercise book. From what you have learned about doctors so far, where would you place them on this line? Be prepared to justify your thinking in a discussion.

Totally ineffective ⟵————————⟶ Very effective

❸ Think about some of the simple illnesses that we have today:
   a fever
   b common cold
   c asthma
   d headache

For each of these, which of the four humours do you think a medieval doctor might suggest are out of balance?

Crazy cures?

Medieval doctors believed that a person's star sign would have an effect on their health throughout their life. At your birth, the best place for a doctor to be was not in the room helping with the delivery, but at the window logging the precise position of the stars and planets.

Why did doctors have these views? What was missing from their knowledge?

The causes of disease

Medieval doctors firmly believed that disease was caused by one of three things:

- **bad air**
- **contagion** (contact with an ill person)
- **a punishment from God**

Doctors' cures tended to reflect this belief in logic. If they knew the cause, their cure should be able to reverse or counteract the cause. For example, if the disease was caused by bad air then the cure would be to change the air.

By today's standards these cures do not sound particularly logical. Medieval doctors had no means of understanding what really caused disease; they had no idea about germs.

Activity

❶ Look at the list of 'cures' in the table below. Can you link the causes of the illnesses with the cures used? Copy the table into your exercise book and complete it by ticking the relevant boxes.

Cure	Bad air	Contagion	God's punishment
Get a blessing from the local priest			
Light fires of sweet-smelling juniper branches			
Lock yourself away in confinement for 5 days			
Walk through the streets of your town whipping yourself as a way of gaining forgiveness			
Carry herbs in a pouch around your neck			

❷ Make up your own cure for an illness and design the label for its bottle. It will need to show clearly what the ingredients are and what condition it is supposed to help.

'Magic' remedies

Today many people have their own 'cures' for minor ailments. Some people may believe, for example, that going to bed with a hot drink of orange squash and a spoonful of honey will cure a common cold, or gargling with a vinegary relish will cure a sore throat.

Medieval doctors had similar ideas. Their most common treatments for illness were **herbal remedies**, which in some people's eyes bordered on magic. Many doctors even referred to their cures as **potions**.

Look at the list of cures that were commonplace in the Middle Ages (**Source A**).

Bleeding

Some doctors would even slice open a vein and let the patient bleed — for a short time at least — catching measured amounts in a **bleeding cup**. If they were squeamish they might have used bloodsucking **leeches** instead to do the job for them.

Bleeding a patient

Bleeding was often used as a cure, especially for fevers where the sufferer was too hot. Look back at the 'Theory of the four humours' on page 57. You can see that the idea was to make sure that the humours were back in balance. Too much blood was a problem during a fever, so doctors bled the patient to bring the humours back into equilibrium.

Source A

Illness	Cure
Headache	Place a ripe goat's cheese on the patient's head.
Toothache	Tie a leather necklace with the beak of a magpie around the neck of the sufferer.
Eye infection	Place a pounded onion under the eye until tears start.
Stomach ache	After 2 days of fasting, eat oat and wheat gruel mixed with honey.
Sprains	Wrap sweetly scented comfrey (a plant) leaves around the affected area and leave for 5 days.

Thinking aloud

There seems to be an element of superstition in some of these ideas, and yet some herbal remedies actually worked.

❖ Why might that be?
❖ Which of the remedies mentioned in **Source A** might still be used today?

A good medieval surgeon

A medieval amputation

There was another branch of medicine at this time, a far more dangerous and deadly art: **surgery**.

Barber-surgeons

The role of barber-surgeons was completely separate from that of doctors. For a start, their main job was that of a barber.

They cut hair and also performed minor surgical operations for poorer people from the safety of their own shops.

Surgeons' skills

These surgeons needed a different range of skills from those of normal doctors. These skills included removing teeth,

lancing boils, excising (cutting out) growths and the worst job of all, amputations. You needed a strong stomach to be in this line of work.

Surgeons, who had to train for at least 7 years, needed to be skilful with a knife and to be used to the sight and smell of fresh blood. They also needed keen eyesight and strong arms to saw through human bones, muscles and sinews (operations could take a while). They had a calendar of 'lucky' days on which they felt it was better to operate.

Drawbacks

There was a major problem in going to see a surgeon and undergoing an operation: there was no such thing as **anaesthetic**, although there was some experimentation with different herbal potions that could send people to sleep — sometimes for ever! There was no **antiseptic** either. Some surgeons used to wash out wounds with wine, but their equipment was often filthy. They thought that a bloodstained overall might make people more confident that their surgeon was experienced.

A barber-surgeon at work

Fact box

The red and white poles that are seen outside barbers' shops today come from the bloody bandages that barbers used to hang outside their shops to drum up trade.

Activity

❶ Make a **memory map** for a surgeon's life. A memory map should summarise the key points in one or two words. Those words should be written in bold along horizontal lines at the end of each branch of the map. Give each branch a different colour that you can connect with the image or facts. You could add a simple picture to help you recall each key point. Remember that it has to make sense to you and it must be easily readable.

❷ Design a job advert for a medieval doctor. Stress the qualities he would need.

❸ It is time to make your second decision about the effectiveness of medieval doctors. Look at the 'Totally ineffective/Very effective' line from page 57 that you filled in earlier. From what you have learned about doctors now, where would you place them on this line? Is it different from your first decision? If so , why?

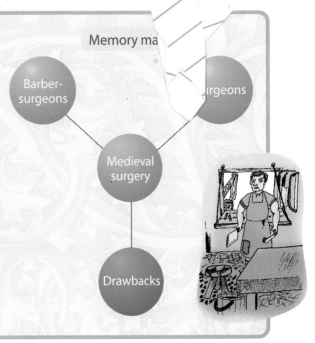

Memory map

- Barber-surgeons
- surgeons
- Medieval surgery
- Drawbacks

The Black Death

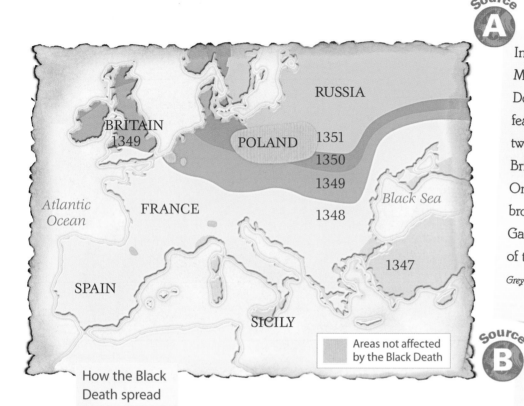

How the Black Death spread

Source A

In this year, 1348, in Melcombe in the county of Dorset, a little before the feast of St John the Baptist, two ships, one of them from Bristol, came alongside. One of the sailors had brought with him from Gascony (France) the seeds of the terrible pestilence…

Grey Friar's Chronicle, Lynn

Source B

Wretched, terrible, destructive year, the remnants of the people alone remain.

This inscription, carved on a tomb in 1349 at St Mary's church, Ashwell, Hertfordshire, was one man's response to a disease that had reached Britain only 1 year before

The Black Death spread to London in 1348, then to Wales and Ireland (1349) and finally Scotland (1350). This rapid spread of the plague reveals that it was easily transmitted.

The two forms of the plague

The two main forms of the disease had different ways of being passed from person to person:

❖ **Bubonic plague:** the bacteria were carried in the bloodstream of rats.

They infected fleas, which bit people and infected them. It was worst in the flea-infested summer months. Over 70% of those infected died a horrible death in 4–7 days.

❖ **Pneumonic plague:** passed on by victims coughing blood and spraying spittle when they breathed out. It was present all year round and over 90% of those infected died within 2 days.

The spread of the disease in crowded towns and villages, where people did not know

how it was transmitted, was devastating. Death rates varied greatly. For example, 19% of villagers died at Hartlebury in the West Midlands, but 80% died at Aston. **Sources A** and **B** describe the spread and effect of the Black Death.

The *danse macabre*. The death throes and corpses of plague victims played on the imagination of artists

❶ Draw a simple flow diagram to show how people caught the Black Death and how it affected them.

❷ Rearrange the statements below to re-create your own story of how the plague spread. Use the blank boxes to add extra statements from the map or the text.

a In Messina, Sicily, in 1347, 12 galleys arrived with sailors who infected all they spoke to.

b In 1343 the plague had reached the Black Sea port of Kaffa, in the Crimea.

c In 1349 Wales, then Ireland, recorded deaths due to the plague.

d In the autumn of 1348 London was affected.

e The records of a cemetery in Issyk Kul (Kyrgyzstan) indicate there were three plague victims in 1338–39.

f In 1350 Scottish invaders plundering northern England found they were infected when they returned home.

g

h

Fact or fiction?

Some people think the Black Death was so called because in some cases infected areas turned black with blood from internal bleeding. Others say it is a misunderstanding of the Latin expression for the plague: *pestis atra* or *atra mors*. *Atra* is translated as dreadful/terrible but can also mean black.

Thinking aloud

With the medical knowledge we have today it may seem incredible to us that medieval people failed to stop the spread of the Black Death, or plague. But is it so strange when modern medicine has no real way of stopping the spread of AIDS or Asian bird flu?

People's reactions

People turned to the doctors, who had no effective cures (see **Source C**). Many became ultra-religious, even beating themselves to make up for any wrongs they imagined an angry god could punish them for (see picture below). Others doubted the existence of a god that could allow this to happen. Paintings (such as the *danse macabre* pictured on page 63) and carvings began to show a fascination with death. The space between the dead and the living seemed very small.

Source C

Black Death signs	Black Death 'cures'
✤ Swellings ('buboes') on infected limbs ✤ Purplish-black patches on the skin ✤ Fever and coughing of blood ✤ Rash	✤ Wash patient in vinegar and water ✤ Cut open buboes to let out disease, then smear with ointment of lilies and human excrement ✤ Bleed patient ✤ Eat more bread, fruit and vegetables ✤ Drink a mix of eggshells, marigolds, treacle and ale ✤ Place a live hen next to swelling and drink own urine every day

In some countries people beat themselves in the hope that God would forgive them for sins they believed they were being punished for

The people who benefited

Some people benefited from the plague. Survivors found they could command higher prices for their labour and buy goods, or even land, cheaply. In some areas ploughmen's wages increased by five times.

With between 30% and 45% of the population dead, demand for goods was reduced so prices fell, making the wealth of survivors go further.

For some landlords the plague removed the numerous tenants they didn't want.

The changes to society were far-reaching, but within 70 years it is estimated that England had replaced half of the population it had lost.

Activity

❶ Suggest why the cures in **Source C** and the following 'solutions' had little success:

  a In some countries, including Germany, people beat themselves (flagellation) in the hope that God would forgive them for the sins they imagined they were being punished for.

  b In some cities, like London and Florence, the authorities ordered the cleansing of the streets by disposing of rubbish and human filth.

  c In Strasbourg, Jewish people were burned as they were thought to have poisoned the water supply.

❷ Write a paragraph to suggest why some historians think the Black Death was not a dreadful end to life in Britain, but rather a temporary setback.

What had to change to improve medicine?

1 The Catholic Church forbade any cutting up of the human body.

14 People were superstitious, especially when it came to new things.

13 Some people thought that the heart moved around the body.

12 Herbal remedies could not cure certain illnesses.

11 There were no quick means of travel.

2 Communication was difficult in medieval times — there were few roads and no telephones.

Problems related to medicine in medieval times

10 It took at least 7 years of training to become a doctor.

Few people could read or write in medieval times. **9**

3 Nobody had ever seen a human skeleton.

4 Nobody seemed to know that blood was pumped around the body.

5 Ancient medical knowledge was written in books in Latin.

6 A number of wars were fought in the Middle Ages. There was a lot of killing.

7 Hospitals were run by monks and nuns and were more like hotels for weary travellers than hospitals.

Peasants in the country-side often shared their homes with their animals. **8**

Activity

How could things ever get better?

❶ Make a full page copy of the concept diagram in your exercise book.

❷ Read the problems listed above and place the statements or their numbers alongside the concept or the linking lines where you think they fit best.

❖ Which of the problems were to do with a lack of education? Put these near the 'Knowledge' section of your diagram.

❖ Do the same for 'War', 'Religion' and 'Superstition'.

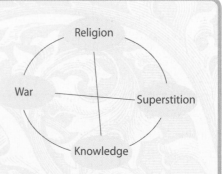

Religion

War

Superstition

Knowledge

❸ Which problem do you think did most to stop medical knowledge progressing?

❹ Did any of these problems have a **positive** effect on the future knowledge of doctors?

How fair was the English legal system in the Middle Ages?

In medieval times there were many different courts to try people for the crimes they had committed.

Manorial courts

If peasants committed a crime they were tried by their lord. The trial would take place at a manorial court; these courts were controlled by the local barons. As most people were peasants, this was the most common type of court.

The trials were held at the manor house and the people who gathered the evidence and took the decisions about who was guilty and who was not were the jury. The jury was made up of 12 villeins chosen by the rest of the village.

The lord, who presided over these courts, could keep the fines he collected. No wonder lords were keen to see law and order upheld.

Look at the following list of crimes. With a partner, try to put them in order of importance. Put the most serious crime first and the least serious crime last.

a Failure to pay your council tax

b Failure to pay off your credit card bill

c Murder

d Murder of a priest

e Theft of a loaf of bread

f Theft of a sheep

g Mugging

h Parking your car on double yellow lines

What makes some crimes more serious than others? What matters most — what the crime is or who it is committed against?

Were there any offences that you thought were equally serious? Were there any crimes that were not really all that serious?

If you were walking down the street and someone shouted 'Stop! Thief!' at someone running straight towards you, would you try to stop them? Explain your answer.

Do you think you have a duty to help the rest of the community to stop crime, or is it someone else's responsibility?

King's courts

More serious crimes, like treason committed by knights and barons, were tried in the king's courts. The trials were usually held with the king in attendance as the judge.

Church courts

These were controlled by the Church, where bishops could try priests and monks who committed crimes. It was this sort of court that Thomas Becket was so keen to keep, and part of the reason he fell out with Henry II (see pages 19–21).

(see pages 19–21)

Activity

❶ Which courts would the following people be tried in?
- a A knight who had failed to pay his taxes to his baron
- b A villein who had failed to pay his taxes to his baron
- c A villein who had been found robbing his neighbour
- d A baron who had been plotting a rebellion
- e A villein who had been plotting a rebellion
- f A knight who had murdered a priest
- g A priest who had killed one of his congregation

❷ Divide a double page in your exercise book into ten equal squares. In three of the squares you are going to design a definition for each of the types of court: manorial, king's and Church. There is a catch, however. You *cannot use any words* at all — only pictures or symbols to help you produce a clear definition. The definitions should be clear enough for your partner to be able to guess which one is which. You can place them in any three of the ten squares, as this is going to be a test for your partner at the end.

The king hearing a law suit

Trials in the Middle Ages

Choosing the right court for the trial was relatively simple, but as you have seen (in Topic 3) some kings and churchmen fell out over this.

Jury duties

There were other problems for those involved in the justice system, particularly in the manorial courts. Those chosen to be on the **jury** had to find the evidence, present it to the court and then decide on the person's guilt or innocence. They also had to make sure that everyone in the village attended the trials; the jury was responsible for fining the people who did not come.

Tithings

Everyone in the village was expected to be involved in this system of justice. All the men of the village were grouped into **tithings** (groups of ten men), who were responsible for making sure that all their members obeyed the laws. If one person in a tithing broke the law, the other nine were responsible for getting him to court and facing his judgement. If the tithing failed to do this, the members paid a fine.

If the person did go to court, the others in the tithing were expected to guarantee that he would not be in trouble again. If he misbehaved, the *others* were fined.

Hue and cry

Public involvement in preventing crime went even further. If a crime was committed and the victim shouted for help, everyone had to help the victim and try to find the criminal. It was known as raising the **hue and cry**. If people did not help they were liable to appear in court themselves.

Trials by ordeal

The picture opposite shows another vital part of the legal system in medieval times. The king's court sometimes opted for **trial by ordeal**. Under this method the court was putting its trust not in the king or his appointed judges to decide a person's innocence or guilt, but in God. The Church courts also often used ordeals to try people. The three main ordeals involved were:
- trial by hot iron or hot water
- trial by cold water
- trial by battle

Activity

❶ Look at the following statements:
a The lord was the main source of law and order in his manor.
b The villeins were the main victims of the manorial courts.
c The jury was vital in making sure that the trial was fair.

Write down all three statements, saying whether you agree or disagree with each one, and find a piece of factual evidence to back up your decision.

❷ Some people tried to get out of serving on the jury in their local village. Can you think of **three** reasons why this might be so?

❸ Some historians describe this system of laws as one of 'collective responsibility'. Explain what you think this phrase might mean.

❹ Design a set of three more definitions to add to the previous three on the double page you started before, to show the terms 'hue and cry', 'tithings' and 'jury'. The same rules apply as before — no words, only pictures or symbols to convey your definition. These can be placed anywhere in your seven remaining squares, as this is going to be a test for your partner at the end.

Trial by hot iron or hot water

The accused had to pick up a piece of red-hot metal, or reach into a boiling cauldron to retrieve an object. His hands were then bandaged for a few days. If the wounds were healed, the person was deemed to be innocent.

Trial by cold water

The accused had a rope tied around his waist and was dunked into cold water, for example in the local pond. If the person was innocent he would sink into the water. He might drown, but he would still be innocent. If he floated, he was guilty.

Trial by battle

The accused and the accuser fought each other. The person who won the duel to the death was deemed to be innocent. This particularly brutal method was introduced by the Normans, who decreed that any man had the right to defend himself with his body against any accuser, until death or until one or other confessed. The picture below shows a trial by battle.

By 1215 ordeals were outlawed by the Magna Carta, which guaranteed the idea of a fair trial. But, as can be seen here, it was still possible to opt for trial by battle in some cases.

Activity

❺ Why might Church courts be keen to use the ordeals as a method of trying people?

❻ It is time to add another three entries to your picture definitions. This time you need to work out some visual definitions for the three trials by ordeal, 'trial by hot iron or hot water', 'trial by cold water' and 'trial by battle'. Remember, no words, only pictures or symbols, and they can be placed anywhere in the four squares that are left.

Trial by battle

Who checked laws were obeyed?

As we have seen, there were a number of people involved in the medieval legal system, from the king and important churchmen down to the lowly jurors.

The people who tried to stop the crimes in the first place were the villeins. They had to respond to the hue and cry and were responsible for nine other villeins through the system of tithings.

But other people were involved too. Low-paid helpers, like the **constables**, could arrest people or break up fights. Volunteers, like the **watchmen**, tended to patrol at night to make sure that the streets were peaceful.

The curfew

Patrolling the streets was an easier job than it seems, as most people obeyed the **curfew** and stayed in their houses after nightfall. The curfew was another Norman invention, which was first introduced during the rebellions of 1067–71. It made sure that people could not meet and plot together to overthrow the king.

Source A

A judge: he decides on the sentence and gives rulings on legal matters

A witness box: the defendant is giving evidence

A modern-day courtroom

The 'King's or Queen's Bench': the seat the judge sits on

A barrister: he is presenting a case of either guilt or innocence

Activity

❶ Now you need to fill in the last box on your double page of definitions. This time you can choose one term to illustrate from the following: 'constable', 'watchman' or 'curfew'. Remember, no words, only pictures or symbols.

❷ Once you have completed this, you can either swap books and get your partner to identify the definitions from your pictures, or you can describe the pictures to see if your partner can guess the correct definitions. You cannot use the keywords in your descriptions.

❸ Look at **Source A**, a picture of a modern-day courtroom. List any differences and similarities between a medieval and a modern trial such as that pictured here.

Other features of a modern-day courtroom not visible in the illustration include:
❖ the jury who are selected and decide on whether a person is innocent or guilty
❖ the Public Gallery where anyone can go and watch the trial
❖ the Press Gallery where the news reporters can watch the trial
❖ the Court Usher who 'swears in' the witnesses
❖ solicitors who offer advice to their clients
❖ the royal coat of arms which is there to remind everyone that the law is the queen's or king's

Overview activity

❶ It is now time to make your mind up about the medieval system of justice, to answer the question 'Could you get a fair trial in medieval England?' Some possible paragraph headings (not in order) are:
❖ Conclusion
❖ The jury
❖ Ordeals
❖ Evidence
❖ Introduction
❖ The judge

Conclusion	The jury	Evidence
Ordeals	Introduction	The judge

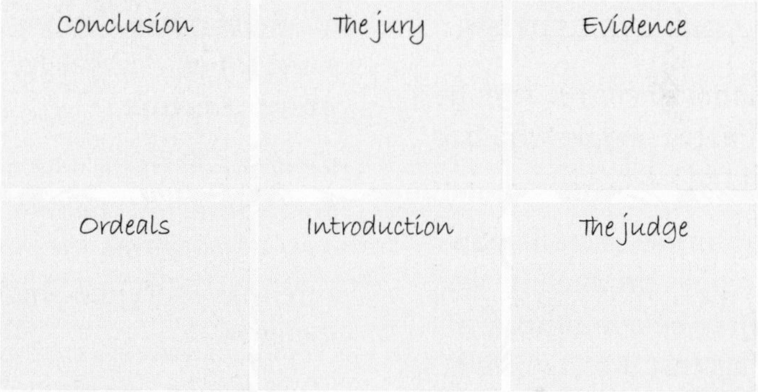

❷ Make six cards containing the above headings as the points of the report you are going to make on the medieval trial system.

❖ Start by explaining briefly on the introduction card what you think.

❖ Write down two pieces of evidence for each of the four points ('The jury', 'Ordeals', 'Evidence' and 'The judge') to show whether it was easier or harder to get a fair trial in medieval times than it is nowadays. If you find you have two pieces of evidence proving that it was possible to get a fair trial, then this factor can be used to prove that case. If you have one piece of evidence to prove it was possible and one to prove that it was not, you will have to judge for yourself which is the more important of the two points.

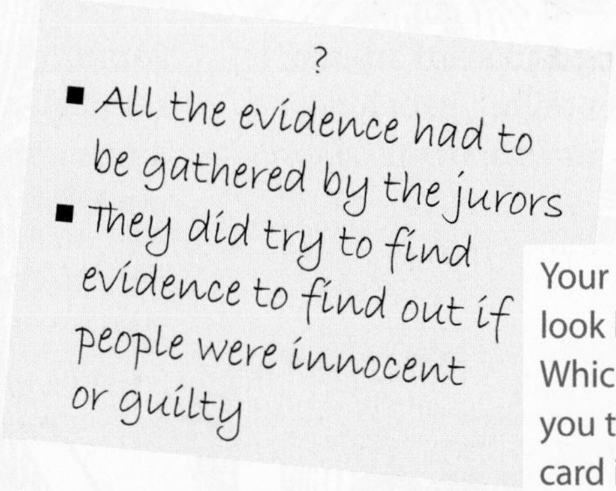

?
■ All the evidence had to be gathered by the jurors
■ They did try to find evidence to find out if people were innocent or guilty

Your cards might look like this. Which factor do you think this card is giving the reasons for?

❖ The next step is easier. You need to organise your paragraphs into the best order to write up your report. So if a card has two points showing that it was possible to get a fair trial and you want to prove that in your report, you could use that as your first paragraph, after your introduction.

❖ Finally, on the conclusion card, explain why you have reached your decision.

❖ Think back to the essay you wrote in Topic 1 on whether or not William the Conqueror was a good leader (page 9). You can use PEEBS success criteria to help you again.

Did the punishment fit the crime?

In medieval times people thought it was important to try to link the punishment to the crime.

Less serious crimes

The manorial courts were best placed to try people who had committed petty crimes.

If, for example, a craftsman made a poor product, he was thought to be committing a crime against the townsfolk. He would therefore have to have a punishment such as carrying a placard around the streets telling people what a poor craftsman he was.

This **humiliation** was meant to do two things: it showed which people were criminals and it also acted as a warning to others not to do the same thing — it was to **prevent crime**.

Remember, there was no police force. All people were responsible for making sure that everyone abided by the laws.

More serious crimes

Some crimes were much more serious and so were tried in the king's court. As a result, the punishments were harsher.

Persistent thieves tended to be tried in the king's court. It was not unknown for thieves to be sentenced to the amputation of a hand (although you could be sentenced to the same punishment in the manorial courts for poaching the lord's game — even wild

Stocks

rabbits that lived on his land were his).

For very serious crimes like treason (plotting against the king) there was only one punishment that would fit the crime: death. (Look back at King Richard II and the peasants who rebelled against him in Topic 3.)

Public punishments

All the above punishments were public. They were there to remind people what the laws were and what the consequences of wrongdoing would be.

Ducking stool

1 Look at the crimes in the list below. As you did for the list of modern-day crimes at the start of this topic, put these in order of most serious to least serious.

a A man out on the street after the curfew

b A woman selling rotten apples at her market stall

c A man found next to the dead body of a wealthy man

d A poor man found with a sack full of fine cloth

e A man who has refused to pay the taxes to his lord

f An old woman who has been accused of being a witch

2 Which of these crimes do you think might have been settled by a trial by ordeal?

Hanging

3 Now look at the pictures of medieval punishments. These, and the list below, show some of the more common punishments given out by the courts in medieval times.

a Having one's ear cut off *or* tongue cut out *or* eyes gouged out

b Being exiled (made to leave) or thrown over the town walls and told to stay away from the town

c Having one's forehead branded with the letter 'T' for 'Thief'

d Being pardoned by the lord or the king

e Having one's nose slit in two (this led to the expression 'paying through the nose')

f Being whipped in the market square

Can you match up the crimes in Activity 1 with these punishments? Remember, punishments were meant to **fit the crimes**.

4 Some punishments were designed specifically for certain crimes.

a Which one of the punishments was designed for people who did not *pay* their tax bill?

b Which punishment was designed for people who started *idle gossip*?

c People who *listened* to the gossip got punished too. Which punishment do you think they received?

d What might happen to people who refused to give their *eyewitness* account at a trial?

5 Look at the following crimes and decide what the punishment for each should be.

a Assaulting a traveller in a forest

b Fighting with a monk over food

c Robbery with a weapon

d Being a member of a gang of criminals

e Being the leader of a gang of criminals, on the run

f Kidnapping

g Attempting to murder a legal official, e.g. a sheriff

h Attempting to overthrow the king

Who was Robin Hood?

The last activity you did on page 73, on thinking of punishments for a list of crimes was referring to Robin Hood. Without discussing your ideas with anyone, draw a picture to show what you think Robin Hood looked like. Take a full page in your exercise book. If you are not confident about your drawing skills you could write labels to describe parts of the drawing.

You should include the following:
- colours, if possible
- Robin doing something
- his location
- any special clothing or equipment that he might have
- an approximate date of when he lived

Hero or hardened criminal?

Robin Hood is usually regarded as a hero in the stories that you read about him, but the list of his crimes on page 73 casts him in a very different light. He appears to have been a common criminal who plotted treason against the king.

Such differing views in the study of history are referred to as **interpretations**. Read the story that follows. It is based on the traditional story of Robin Hood.

1   A long time ago in the County of Nottinghamshire, at a place called **Locksley**, **Robert Fitzooth** is born, an heir to the **Earl of Huntingdon**'s land.

2   The earl has a powerful enemy in the shape of **King John**, who is ruling England while his brother **Richard I**, the Lionheart, is away fighting in the Crusades in the Middle East. King John is determined to seize as much land as he can while his brother is away, and he takes the earl's land after falsely accusing him of treason.

3 The earl is killed and his son, now known as **Robert of Locksley**, is declared an **outlaw**. This means he could be killed and his killer would not be charged with murder because Robert is living outside the protection of the law. So he runs away to the forest and changes his name to Robin Hood. He determines to fight King John in whatever way he can.

4 Robin finds several other outlaws who are opposed to King John. He meets **Little John** on a small bridge over a stream in the forest. Neither man will give way and the pair fight with staffs (long sticks). Little John knocks Robin into the water. He is immediately recruited into Robin Hood's band of **Merry Men**, and becomes Robin's best friend.

5 **Friar Tuck** is another character who joins the Merry Men after Robin chances upon him in the forest. Tuck is forced to carry Robin across the river. The monk does it, but throws Robin in the water and forces Robin to carry him back across. They too become good friends and others gradually join them, like **Will Scarlet** and **Mutch the Miller's Son**. They manage to live in the forest by hunting the king's deer and robbing the richer travellers who pass through.

6 Robin and his men are always ready to help out the poor and needy, however. Sometimes they give money, for example to a poor knight, **Sir Richard of the Lea**, who has to pay off a huge debt he owes to the Church. Sometimes Robin Hood and his followers have to fight against the supporters of King John, particularly the **Sheriff of Nottingham**.

7 The sheriff and his men are the constant target of Robin and his followers. The sheriff cannot control the forest, and Robin's men continue to rob the rich travellers. When the sheriff's men try to arrest Robin they are ambushed, stripped of their clothes and sent back out of the forest, embarrassed, much to the amusement of the Merry Men.

8

In a devious attempt to trap Robin, the sheriff, egged on by King John, arranges an archery competition. The prize is a golden arrow, for the best archer in England. Robin enters, just so that he can see **Matilda**, his childhood sweetheart, who is to give the prize to the winner. Robin faces a stiff challenge from another archer who strikes the target with a bull's-eye, but Robin wins the tournament by firing an arrow that splits the other archer's arrow in two. When Matilda presents the prize the sheriff recognises Robin and has him arrested.

9

Robin is held prisoner at Nottingham Castle and is sentenced, by King John himself, to hang. Robin's cause seems lost as a cart takes him to the gallows. But as the noose is slipped around his neck, an arrow fired by one of the Merry Men severs the rope and Robin is rescued by Little John on horseback. The pair ride out of the gates of Nottingham Castle to the safety of Sherwood.

10

Robin's arch enemy is **Sir Guy of Guisburne**, a ruthless Norman knight who tries to steal the Earl of Fitzwalter's daughter, Matilda (the childhood sweetheart of Robin, who wants to marry her himself). Guisburne swears to kill Robin. Matilda doesn't want Guisburne as she is in love with Robin, and she runs away to the forest. There she lives with Robin and the Merry Men and changes her name to **Marian**.

11

All is well until one day when a party of monks comes into Sherwood Forest, searching for Robin. They are captured and are about to be robbed, when the monks reveal themselves to be knights back from the Crusades. One of them is, in fact, the rightful king, Richard I, who pardons Robin and gives him his lands back.

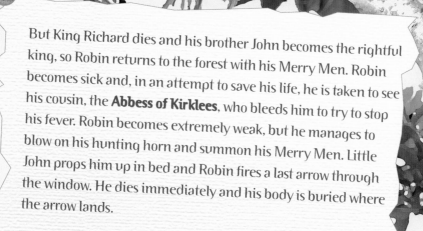

But King Richard dies and his brother John becomes the rightful king, so Robin returns to the forest with his Merry Men. Robin becomes sick and, in an attempt to save his life, he is taken to see his cousin, the **Abbess of Kirklees**, who bleeds him to try to stop his fever. Robin becomes extremely weak, but he manages to blow on his hunting horn and summon his Merry Men. Little John props him up in bed and Robin fires a last arrow through the window. He dies immediately and his body is buried where the arrow lands.

Activity

❶ Look at the list of names below. Divide a page into two columns. You are going to arrange the names into two sides. On one side of the page put people who are on Robin Hood's side and on the other side put people who are against him.
  a Will Scarlet
  b Sir Richard of the Lea
  c Sir Guy of Guisburne
  d Mutch the Miller's Son
  e King John
  f Little John
  g Matilda
  h King Richard I
  i Friar Tuck
  j the Sheriff of Nottingham
  k the Earl of Huntingdon

❷ The story is very exciting and quite complicated. It would make an excellent film (there have been quite a few made already). Below are four possible scenes:

  a King Richard the Lionheart returns in disguise.
  b Robin meets Little John on the bridge in Sherwood Forest.
  c Robin loses his land and is forced to become an outlaw in the forest.
  d Robin is imprisoned in Nottingham Castle.

Rearrange the scenes so that they are in the correct chronological order.

❸ If you were going to make a storyboard of this for a film, what other four scenes might you use? Remember, a storyboard picks the most dramatic or exciting scenes to tell the story. Write the titles for each of the four scenes.

❹ Now you have a choice: *either* draw the eight pictures of the storyboard for the whole film; *or* write a script for one of the more dramatic scenes, to show how the drama might unfold in the words that the characters might use.

Whichever option you choose, try to make it authentic by taking care not to rely on anything that would not have been around at the time.

❺ Are there any parts of the story that you think are a little far-fetched, or that may be inaccurate? Make a list of any parts of the story that do not fit with your knowledge of medieval life.

What did Robin Hood really look like?

Inference grid

What questions do I need to ask about Robin Hood?

What doesn't it tell us about Robin Hood?

What does the picture tell us about Robin Hood?

This is in black and white; what colours did he wear?

It doesn't show whether he killed any animals or not.

He had a hunting horn.

His hat had a feather in it.

ROBIN HOOD

Starter activity

Look at this image of Robin Hood from 1912. It gives us a lot of information about Robin. It also raises some interesting questions. Copy the inference grid into your exercise book and fill in as much detail as you can.

Activity

❶ Earlier in this topic you drew a picture to show what you thought Robin Hood looked like. It is now time to compare your drawing with the images on these pages (including the one in the inference grid). Copy and complete the following table. Add the analysis of your own picture last.

What similarities are there between the pictures? What differences are there?

Picture	Brief description	Similarities to other pictures	Differences from other pictures
B	Shows a man on horseback.	He has a bow and arrow. He is wearing a hat. He has spurs, so might be a knight.	He is riding a horse.

❷ Looking at all the pictures, what answers could you give to the following questions?
  a What equipment did Robin Hood **definitely** carry?
  b What clothes did he **definitely** wear?
  c What skills did Robin Hood **definitely** have?
  d How do you know?

❸ There are many pictures of Robin Hood, but no contemporary drawing of him has survived. The earliest is picture A. Is this the most **reliable** picture of what Robin Hood looked like? Explain your answer.

Could a person like Robin Hood have existed?

So far we have looked at the traditional view of Robin Hood, both of his life story and of his appearance. To be able to judge whether a person like Robin could have existed, we need to consider a range of other evidence. As you read through the following information, decide whether it proves that such a person could have existed or not.

Robert was a common man's name in medieval times.

The name Robert was often 'shortened' to Robin.

People who didn't attend court were said to be living outside the protection of the law, so they were 'outlaws'.

King Richard I (the Lionheart) ruled England from 1189 to 1199.

It was the law of the land that every man should own a longbow and be prepared to defend the king whenever required.

Sheriffs and monks were often the people who collected taxes in the medieval era.

Richard the Lionheart was out of the country on the Third Crusade from 1189 to 1192.

Groups of outlaws often sought refuge in forests as a way of hiding from the law.

The surname Hood was common in medieval times.

Outlaws could be killed on sight.

Richard the Lionheart had a brother called John, who ruled England from 1199 to 1216.

The name Robert Hood appeared in the court records at Wakefield Court in Yorkshire in 1322.

Sir Thomas Thwing was an outlaw from Yorkshire who was known to rob from the rich and give to the poor, in the 1230s.

A man called Robin Hood was arrested in Northamptonshire in 1354 for poaching in a royal forest.

In the 1380s a band of outlaws, who used bows and arrows, lived in a forest and were led by a man called William Beckwith.

Piers Venables was a criminal in Derbyshire who was compared with 'the rascal Hood'.

People who carried out robberies often wore a robe and hood to cover their face in medieval times.

There are nine places called 'Robin Hood's Butts' dotted around England, as far apart as Cumbria in the northwest and Devon in the southeast.

There is a gravestone of a Robin Hood in Hathersage, in Derbyshire.

There are three other graves of Robin Hood: one in the old forest at Sherwood, near Mansfield in Nottinghamshire; one near Wakefield in West Yorkshire; and another in Cumbria.

There was a huge royal forest at Barnesdale in Yorkshire.

Ballads about an outlaw called Robin Hood appeared in 1456.

Thieves and highway robbers were often referred to in medieval times as 'robe and hood' criminals.

Activity

❶ You need to make a decision about whether it was *possible* for a man like Robin Hood to have existed in medieval times. There is a great deal of evidence to sort out.

Read each piece of information and decide which one of the four boxes it belongs in. Copy the following table onto a double page in your exercise book and complete it.

This evidence shows that it **was probable**.	This evidence shows that it **could be possible**.
This evidence shows that it **could not be possible**.	This evidence shows that it **was not likely**.

An alternative way

Another way of sorting out the information could be to collect together all the evidence that is to do with:

✤ Robin Hood's name   ✤ where he lived

✤ what he did   ✤ when he lived

You could draw another table as above, but change the categories to these new ones.

❷ Look at the two statements below. Using all the evidence you have and your own opinion, which statement best reflects your **interpretation**? (If you don't agree entirely with either of them, whereabouts on the line would your opinion come?)

Robin Hood never existed; he was a character that story-telling minstrels made up to entertain people with.

Robin Hood was a famous criminal who was imitated by others, throughout the ages, and the story grew as a result.

❸ Try to think of two other statements that you could put at either end of the line that could also be true according to different **interpretations** of the evidence.

❹ Work out which is the best way to sort your information and then answer the question:

Was it possible for a man like Robin Hood to have existed in medieval times?

Was this still the age of kings?

This book has focused on events in medieval times that were significant in our opinion. By choosing the events that we did we had to make a judgement. We are now going to try to sum up the period and the things that happened. First of all, we are going to look at what happened to the power of monarchs over the whole of the medieval period.

The signing of the Magna Carta, 1215

Activity

❶ Make a copy of the graph on a double page in your exercise book. It is going to show the fortunes of the monarchs throughout the period you have studied.

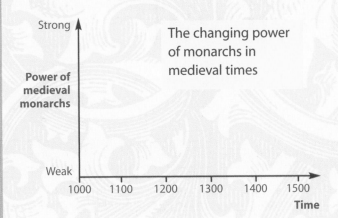

The changing power of monarchs in medieval times

❷ Now you are going to plot your graph. Put an 'X' in the correct places to show whether each event in the list below increased or reduced the power of the monarchy.

a William defeated the Saxon army at Hastings to become the King of England, 1066.

b William the Conqueror made sure that rebellions like Hereward the Wake's were brutally suppressed, 1071.

c England's population had risen to 2.5 million, 1100.

d Henry II asserted his power by having the Archbishop of Canterbury killed, 1170.

e Henry II repented for the killing of Becket, 1174.

f Royal town charters, given to towns by the king as a way of raising funds, became more common, 1190s.

g King John was forced to give in to the demands of the barons at Runnymede and signed the Magna Carta, 1215.

h Simon de Montfort, a baron, began the first Parliament, 1265.

i Edward I conquered Wales, 1295.

j The population of England was 4 million, 1290s.

k William Wallace (the Braveheart) was executed by Edward I, 1305.

l Scotland became independent, 1328.

m About one third of the population was killed by the Black Death, 1348–49.

n The king and his court were threatened in London by the Peasants' Revolt, 1381.

o Rebel peasants were punished by death, 1381.

p The crown of England was fought over by the two warring families of York and Lancaster, 1449.

❸ Look at the shape that your graph has taken. How would you describe what happened to the power of the monarchy throughout the medieval period? Did the power of the monarch increase or decrease? Did the peasants benefit and become more powerful? Or did the barons assert their power over this period? Explain your answer carefully.

❹ Look at the painting of King John and the Magna Carta. Painted in the early twentieth century, this picture hangs in the House of Commons today. It shows a number of things. Try to find the following:

a an advisor to the king offering some late advice

b the broken flagpole and the king's standard in the mud

c a knight carrying his own flag

d a baron from the Crusades (a holy war between Christians and Muslims) threatening the king

e the poor peasants struggling to continue gathering crops for their lords in the fields

f knights with their swords raised against the king

g the churchmen covering themselves up

❺ Look at the picture as a whole. Do you think it is raining raindrops or arrows? Why might the artist have drawn such stormy skies? Do you think that he was trying to create an atmosphere in the picture?

❻ 'This picture sums up the problems that all monarchs faced in the medieval period.' Do you think that this is a fair comment about the kings and their problems?

What was important about the medieval realms?

You have made judgements based solely on the information provided in this book. Would the graph you drew for the activity on page 83 be a different shape if it had used different events? The following activity should make you think more about the judgements you make and encourage you to think more generally about ideas regarding interpretations of the events.

Activity

Look at the following statements and try to decide which is the *best* ending to each sentence.

❶ The Normans found it difficult to gain control of England because…
a …they didn't speak English.
b …there were rebellions all over England.
c …their supplies were all in France.
d …there were some Saxon rebellions in some parts of England.

❷ The Normans imposed their lifestyle on the Saxons by…
a …building great castles all over the country.
b …building magnificent castles and cathedrals all over the country.
c …killing anyone who rebelled against them.
d …writing down everything that people owned in the Domesday Book.

❸ Castles were originally built of wood and were then changed to stone because…
a …wood was cheap and easy to find.
b …wooden castles were quicker to build and they needed them fast.
c …they were often attacked by the Saxons, using fire.
d …the fashions in castle building changed.

❹ Medieval towns were good places to live because…
a …people who lived in them became freemen.
b …it was possible to become a freeman if you lived in a town for a year and a day.
c …strangers were always kept out of them.
d …the guilds often made strict laws for people to live by.

❺ Towns were quite unhealthy places to live because…
a …the streets were full of human filth.
b …nobody who lived in towns really understood the problems of germs and disease.
c …disease spread quickly as the houses were too close together.
d …water supplies were usually polluted.

❻ The king and the Church clashed because…
a …Thomas Becket had tried to get more power for himself.
b …the king had Becket murdered.
c …a lot of kings saw the Church as a threat to their power.
d …the king needed to be the most powerful person in the country to rule it successfully.

7 The Black Death was a very important event in this period because…

  a …it showed how little people really knew about diseases and how they were spread.

  b …it killed off about one third of the population.

  c …it improved the quality of life for the people who survived as their wages went up and they got more to eat.

  d …it showed that some people still believed that God could cause nasty problems for people as a punishment.

8 The legend of Robin Hood is…

  a …an old folk tale that tells of a man who robbed the rich to give to the poor.

  b …about a completely fictional character and is not a proper part of history.

  c …a story about a lot of different people whose characters are put together to give us one person called Robin Hood.

  d …an entertaining story about typical medieval criminals and their antics.

9 By the end of this period, in 1500…

  a …kings were still the most powerful people in the country.

  b …the Church was becoming less important in ordinary people's lives.

  c …kings had lost some of their power but were still important rulers in the country.

  d …the nobles had gained some power from the monarch and the peasants' lives were also getting better.

10 The period 1066–1500 was a time of…

  a knights, castles, plagues and kings.

  b the Church gaining more power.

  c barons gaining more power from the king.

  d kings coming to depend more on the barons to help them rule.

What have you learned?

In each topic of this book you have investigated different aspects of medieval life in Britain. You have also been on a journey from 1066 to 1500. You have learned a lot, but what are the most important events in *your* opinion? Some of the early events you learned about had important effects on the later events. What do *you* think are the links between the key events?

Activity

❶ Make a large copy of the diagram below on a double page in your exercise book or a sheet of A4 paper.

❷ Read back through your notes for each topic shown on the diagram and decide what you think is the single most important fact or event from each topic.

❸ Write it under the topic title on the diagram.

❹ When you have completed it, try to add links between the key facts you have listed.

Hint: the diagram is partially completed, but you may choose other facts or events.

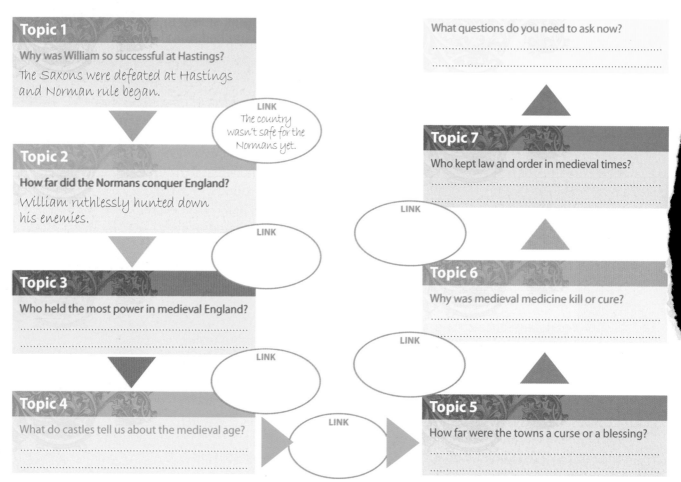

Topic 1

Why was William so successful at Hastings?

The Saxons were defeated at Hastings and Norman rule began.

LINK
The country wasn't safe for the Normans yet.

Topic 2

How far did the Normans conquer England?

William ruthlessly hunted down his enemies.

LINK

Topic 3

Who held the most power in medieval England?

....
....

LINK

Topic 4

What do castles tell us about the medieval age?

....
....

LINK

What questions do you need to ask now?
....
....

Topic 7

Who kept law and order in medieval times?
....
....

LINK

Topic 6

Why was medieval medicine kill or cure?
....
....

LINK

Topic 5

How far were the towns a curse or a blessing?
....
....